Jesse Jackson's Vision for America

BEYOND
OPPORTUNITY

Roger D. Hatch

FORTRESS PRESS   PHILADELPHIA

Second printing 1988

Library of Congress Cataloging-in-Publication Data

Hatch, Roger D.
　Beyond opportunity.

　　1. Jackson, Jesse, 1941–　　—Political and
social views.　2. United States—Politics and
government—1981–　　.　3. United States—Economic
policy—1981–　　.　4. United States—Social
policy—1980–　　.　I. Title.
　E840.8.J35H38　1988　　323.4'092'4　　87–45892
　ISBN 0–8006–2085–2

57,363

3655C88　Printed in the United States of America　1–2085

For all those
who continue to struggle against the headwinds
seeking peace and justice.

Contents

Introduction

American society is currently engaged in an important debate about the meaning and significance of racial justice and civil rights issues, a debate which, in one form or another, has been going on for the past twenty years since the end of the Civil Rights Movement. On one side of this debate is the whole range of traditional civil rights organizations and their friends and allies. They argue that over the centuries racism has become so interwoven in the social and institutional fiber of America that broad, aggressive measures (affirmative actions) are necessary in the political, educational, and economic arenas to root out racism, reverse the current situation, and create a society characterized by racial justice. Jesse Jackson is among the most prominent members of this group, and his entry into national politics has brought his position into full public view.

On the other side at present is the Reagan administration and its friends and allies. They have been arguing for defining "civil rights" in the narrowest possible terms as the strictly legal right of individuals not to be intentionally discriminated against in voting or seeking employment or housing. Accordingly, they claim that mechanisms such as affirmative action and special set-aside programs for minorities are illegitimate because these mechanisms are color-conscious rather than color-blind, and they have repeatedly gone to court to press their claims. Further, they assert that traditional civil rights groups and leaders have strayed from their legitimate roles because they concern themselves with political, economic, educational, and even foreign policy issues rather than with civil rights, narrowly conceived.

1

Many Americans are also engaged in a debate about Jesse Jackson and the meaning and significance of his presence in national politics. Political analysts offered strong, clashing assessments of his 1984 presidential campaign, ranging from the *New Republic's* conclusion that "Jackson has failed to project anything like a coherent vision of a just society at home, which might bind blacks and whites together"[1] to Barry Commoner's claim that Jackson was "giving powerful voice to a comprehensive political program—a rousing return to old-fashioned issue-oriented politics not seen in the Democratic Party since Franklin D. Roosevelt."[2] Some charged that Jackson's campaign was "merely symbolic," unrelated to the real political campaign,[3] while others claimed that "American politics will never be the same."[4]

Although Jesse Jackson has been in the public eye for two decades, Barbara Reynolds's 1975 biography, *Jesse Jackson: The Man, the Movement, the Myth*,[5] has been the only book-length treatment of Jackson available until recently. Since his presidential candidacy in 1984, however, he has been the subject of several books. Thomas H. Landess and Richard M. Quinn draw heavily on Reynolds's work in their book analyzing Jackson's twenty-year public career, *Jesse Jackson and the Politics of Race*.[6] Political scientist Adolph L. Reed, Jr., examines his 1984 campaign in *The Jesse Jackson Phenomenon: The Crisis of Purpose in Afro-American Politics*.[7] Sheila D. Collins also writes about the campaign, but from the standpoint of a participant-observer, in *The Rainbow Challenge: The Jackson Campaign and the Future of U.S. Politics*.[8] Finally, Bob Faw and Nancy Skelton, both reporters who covered him in 1984, chronicle the campaign in *Thunder in America: The Improbable Presidential Campaign of Jesse Jackson*.[9]

Beyond Opportunity is not intended to duplicate the efforts of any of these authors and it employs a different framework to interpret Jackson and his work. Reynolds focuses on Jackson's personality in explaining his activities. Landess and Quinn build on that and then interpret his political activities in the context of the Southern racist populist politics of the 1890–1940 period, arguing that he and his earlier white Southern counterparts attempted "to paint themselves as leaders who had arisen out of the ranks of the oppressed, in order to speak for 'the people' in corrupt political forums controlled by the rich and powerful."[10] Reed focuses on his 1984 campaign, interpreting it in the general context of black electoral politics, and observes that the campaign "was a ritualistic event—a media-conveyed politics of symbolism, essentially tangential to the critical debate over reorganization of American capitalism's governing consensus."[11] Because it was "not so much a political campaign as a crusade,"[12] Reed concludes that Jackson's presidential campaign actually undermined electoral politics within the black community. Faw and Skelton look on his bid for the Democratic party's 1984 presidential nomination as another—although highly interesting and certainly enigmatic—campaign for the presidency. Collins, by contrast, views his 1984 campaign in the context of a variety of twentieth-century movements for social change, which she terms "underground streams in American political life." She concludes: "Jackson's genius lay in linking nonelectoral forms of political mobilization and protest with traditional electoral politics. . . . Although embryonic and fragile, the Rainbow Coalition represents the construction of a new kind of politics appropriate to the history, cultural realities, and changing socioeconomic context of late twentieth-century America."[13]

While each of these interpretive perspectives has some validity and utility, each lies outside of Jackson's own understanding of his political activities, and, indeed, all lie far afield of the institution to which he is most indebted—the black church. James Melvin Washington has examined him from this vantage point in "Jesse Jackson and the Symbolic Politics of Black Christendom."[14] He concludes: "It would be a mistake to conclude that Jesse Jackson is a creation of the news media. His roots are planted deeply within the black church's rich tradition of social, political, and economic activism."[15] This tradition is not simply a black counterpart to the white Christian tradition; it combines religion and politics in a unique way. The examination of Jackson that follows in *Beyond Opportunity* shares Washington's general perspective. To understand Jackson and his activities, one must recognize that it is the black church and the Civil Rights Movement out of which he comes and from which he continues to draw as he moves in the arena of electoral politics. It is in this arena—where religion, politics, and the quest for racial justice come together—that he operates.

From time to time, a political analyst will observe that members of that fraternity ought to be paying attention to what Jesse Jackson is saying, to his ideas, and not just to his personality or his political and rhetorical style. As David Broder noted, "We have paid too little attention to what Jackson is saying. Ultimately, . . . he will be judged by his personal qualities and his record, as well as his ideas. . . . [B]ut the content of what Jackson is saying is obviously important to the nation's political future."[16]

Jackson, however, is not a significant person in American public life primarily because he is a creative thinker; few important political actors are. His creativity lies in his ability to understand and then explain complex issues in simple, direct ways to ordinary people and in his ability to motivate and mobilize people. His mind is agile, and he moves back and forth from abstract ideas to concrete issues with ease and confidence. Yet his way of looking at reality has a coherence and an integrity to it easily missed when viewing a 30-second clip of one of his speeches on the evening news. An examination of his speeches over the years reveals that his statements are more than flippant responses or statements carefully tailored to a particular audience. His statements and his views grow out of a consistent way of looking at reality that is deeply rooted in the black church and in the Civil Rights Movement.

He shares this view of reality with many others influenced by these same organizations. This view, however, has been largely hidden from the majority of Americans over the years because of the veil drawn across American life by racism. Jackson has called this viewing American life "from a black perspective, which is the perspective of the rejected."[17] He goes on to note that "life viewed from a black perspective encompasses more of America than life viewed from a white male middle-class perspective."[18] Until he entered national politics, this view of reality had been largely absent from that arena.

By understanding something of Jesse Jackson and his work and ideas, we gain more, however, than just knowledge about an important and controversial figure in American life. First, we gain some understanding of the unfinished work of the Civil Rights Movement following the passage in 1964 of the Public Accommodations Act and in 1965 of the Voting Rights Act. Eliminating racial injustice in the form of segregation laws has not been sufficient to establish racial justice. He helps us understand what more is required. Second, we gain some understanding of contemporary American electoral politics. His role as an outsider reveals much about the limits of American politics, particularly its racial character and its present failure of vision. Third, we gain some understanding of the creative, sustaining resource that the black church has been and continues to be in American society. As he might say, while the black church examines life from a black perspective, its assets and contributions are not for blacks only.

In *Beyond Opportunity* I will examine Jesse Jackson's basic ideas and his view of reality and interpret his actions in light of them. I have based this study on a comprehensive examination of more than a thousand of his speeches and addresses given over the past two decades. In addition, I served as a member of his staff for six months in 1980, having the opportunity to view him and his activity from close range. Along with Frank E. Watkins, I recently edited *Straight from the Heart,*[19] a collection of Jackson's speeches that he calls "comprehensive" and "representative." Since his speeches in *Straight from the Heart* are the only ones readily available to the public, I have chosen, whenever feasible, to support and illustrate my arguments with citations from speeches that appear there rather than from other sources so that readers may, if they wish, form alternative interpretations of the same materials.

I wish to thank the many people who have contributed to this book: in particular, members of the Social Ethics Seminar and members of the Department of Religion at Central Michigan University, who carefully read and responded to early drafts of several chapters; Dolores Lawrence, Department of Religion Secretary, who graciously took up much of the slack so that I could let several administrative tasks slide in order to work on this volume; the staff at Operation PUSH and the Rainbow Coalition, who allowed ready access to their files; Davis Perkins of Fortress Press, who readily provided advice and assistance throughout the process of writing; Stephanie Egnotovich, Managing Editor of Fortress Press, who skillfully guided the manuscript through the process of editing and publication; Leslie A. Brown, who assisted in the research and typing;

Karen L. Carter, Warren R. Copeland, Ronald R. Primeau, and Frank E. Watkins, who read the entire manuscript and suggested many helpful changes; and Marcia R. Sawyer, who consistently provides that rare combination of personal and professional support and incisive, constructive criticism.

1

Beyond Opportunity

At the core of Jesse Jackson's approach to every aspect of life is a religious-political vision for America. This vision has its roots in the black church—the institution that nurtured him as a child, that helped mold and guide his dreams and ambitions as a young man, and that has sustained and undergirded his work as an adult. While the black church tradition is exceedingly rich and varied, at its base is an affirmation that is both religious *and* political. It is the affirmation that racism is not true, that all human beings are made in God's image and hence have value. Peter J. Paris has put it well: "The fundamental principle of the black Christian tradition is depicted most adequately in the biblical doctrine of the parenthood of God and the kinship of all peoples."[1]

This is a religious principle because it is an affirmation about the very nature of reality, in this case about human nature, human association, and the relation of human beings to God. This principle underlies Jackson's central affirmation—"I am somebody"—and his belief in the interrelated, interdependent nature of reality. This principle (especially the "kinship of all peoples" portion) also provides the basis for criticizing all racist arrangements in society; hence its political as well as religious character. Social policies and social arrangements that deny or devalue the worth of people because of their race are wrong. And it is only by resisting racist arrangements that racially oppressed people can retain their own self-worth.

The history of black people in America shows that blacks have

7

affirmed their own worth by resisting racism in a variety of ways. These forms of resistance have run the gamut from the private intellectual refusal to believe the degrading things that were said to be true about black people to armed attempts to overthrow various institutionalized forms of racism in America, including the federal government.[2] Jackson has chosen the public arena as the one in which he will resist racism.

Jackson has combined the style of a traditional black preacher with some of the brashness of the more secular black power and black pride movement of the late 1960s and early 1970s. Throughout his twenty-year public career, he has kept his eye on the vision of a pluralistic, nonracist society in which people recognize how much they need and depend on one another. However, he is not doctrinaire about which methods must be employed to achieve this vision. He will employ any means available, consistent with the goal he seeks, of making American society less racist and more just. In fact, Jackson urges black Americans to use whatever tools they already have. "We must, without cynicism but with realism, exercise every available . . . option open to us."[3] He argues for a "diversified game plan"[4] and uses the image of an orchestra to point to the many complementary means that must be used when seeking racial justice.[5]

Beyond the religious-political character of his ideas, which is due to their source in the black church, Jackson is by nature a deeply political human being. Roger Wilkins, in an article in *Mother Jones*, described him as "a natural" when it came to politics:

> The main point about Jesse Jackson is not just that he has a fine mind, but that he is to politics what Duke Ellington was to jazz and what Magic Johnson is to basketball. He is a natural. He is nourished by the stuff of politics: the issues, the people, the motion, the turmoil, and the thunder. He is also nourished by his vision of a country that can be better than the one he has known, and by the sense that his efforts can make that vision possible.[6]

Because Jackson's vision, like the central affirmation of the black church tradition, is both religious and political, it is not surprising that his political speeches often contain religious language and imagery and that his sermons usually contain political content. For instance, in announcing his presidential candidacy in 1983, he called for the creation of "new covenants" between the dispossessed and the Democratic party, organized labor, and corporate America,[7] and described his campaign's purpose as "defending the poor, making welcome the outcast, delivering the needy, and being a source of hope for people yearning to be free everywhere."[8] In his campaign speeches, he typically challenged the Democratic party to change, to open itself up to new elements, noting, "Old wineskins must make room for new wine."[9] He offered hope by claiming, "The rejected stones can become the cornerstones of a new progressive coalition in America who will help to reshape a new domestic and world order."[10]

Black churches, regardless of their theological stance, have always addressed politics in one way or another. They have always engaged in social criticism to the extent of repudiating racism in its many embodiments. Sometimes this has taken the form of emphasizing another world in the future and eschewing conventional political involvements. Although this stance often has been viewed as apolitical, the emphasis on another, better world than this one constitutes a powerful indictment and rejection of this world as it is. This view often has been coupled with the judgment that no human activity— be it reform or even revolution—can adequately bring about the kinds of social and political changes necessary to establish justice and peace; it would take the intervention of God.

Leaders in other black churches have argued that conventional political activities are important because they can help establish at least a measure of justice and peace. In this view, religious beliefs about the worth of all people need to be embodied throughout society, not just affirmed in the activities of churches. It was ministers and churches taking this latter stance who became involved in the Civil Rights Movement of the 1950s and 1960s.

JESSE JACKSON

Jesse Jackson, born October 8, 1941, in Greenville, South Carolina, was a high-school and college student during the early years of the Civil Rights Movement.[11] Upon graduation from Sterling High School in Greenville in 1959, Jackson, a star athlete, was offered a chance to try out with a professional baseball team. Jackson, a pitcher, tried out along with a white catcher from Greenville, Dickie Dietz. In the tryout, he struck Dietz out three times. Both were offered contracts, but Dietz was offered $95,000 to sign, Jackson just $6,000. Instead, Jackson chose to attend the University of Illinois on a football scholarship. There he hoped to become the first black quarterback to play in the Big Ten conference. During his freshman year, however, he learned that Illinois would continue to reserve the quarterback position for white athletes; he would have to play another position. Consequently, he transferred after his freshman year to North Carolina A & T, a historically black college in Greensboro, North Carolina, where he eventually became student-body president. Jackson arrived in Greensboro just as the first student sit-ins at Woolworth's lunch counter were beginning and soon became one of the leaders of this movement, which soon spread throughout the country. The sit-ins, coming on the heels of his experiences of discrimination in baseball and football, became one of the crucial, formative experiences in his life.

During his college years in Greensboro, he continued his involvement in various civil rights activities, at one time serving as field director of Southeast operations for CORE, the Congress of Racial Equality, a multiracial group begun in the 1940s which advocated nonviolent direct action, such as sit-ins, to bring about racial justice. His interest in politics (he worked briefly for North Carolina Governor Terry Sanford) led him to consider obtaining a law degree at Duke University. But he experienced God's call to become a minister, and that call finally won out. So he moved north to attend Chicago Theological Seminary in 1963. His interest in politics, however, was not abandoned. Jackson struggled to find an appropriate way to combine his political and religious interests and convictions. As he later observed: "My religion obligates me to be political, that is, to seek to do God's will and allow the spiritual Word to become concrete justice and dwell among us."[12]

When the Southern Christian Leadership Conference (SCLC) headed by Martin Luther King, Jr., began the voting rights campaign in Selma, Alabama, in the spring of 1965, Jackson organized a group of seminary students to make the trip from Chicago to Selma to support the movement. While there, Jackson came to the attention of both Ralph Abernathy, second in command at SCLC, and King. Following the Selma campaign, Jackson returned to Chicago, where he began working for CCCO (the Coordinating Council of Community Organizations), a broad coalition of more than fifty religious, neighborhood, professional, and civic groups working for racial justice in Chicago, particularly in the school system.[13] After the passage of the Voting Rights Act in the summer of 1965, SCLC began its first campaign in the North. It chose Chicago as the site of its activities in part because of CCCO's previous activities. The work of SCLC and CCCO converged and became known as the Chicago Freedom Movement. King rented an apartment on Chicago's West Side and was the most visible leader in this broad-based coalition seeking racial justice. The Chicago Freedom Movement intially focused its work on open housing. This effort in Chicago lasted a little more than a year and culminated in an open-housing agreement with Mayor Richard J. Daley that at best was a compromise, at worst an outright failure for the movement.

Operation Breadbasket, a program to deal with the economic aspects of racial justice already initiated in a few other cities by SCLC, was launched in Chicago in February of 1966, with Jackson among its principal leaders.[14] By the close of SCLC's Chicago campaign in the fall of 1966, Breadbasket was one of the few tangible things SCLC left behind in Chicago. A year later, in August of 1967, King named Jackson Operation Breadbasket's first national director. After King's death in 1968, Ralph Abernathy became King's successor at SCLC. Following several disputes between Abernathy and Jackson, Jackson broke away from SCLC and launched Operation PUSH (People United to Serve Humanity) on Christmas Day of 1971.

PHASE TWO OF THE
CIVIL RIGHTS MOVEMENT

While it could not have been at all clear at the time, Jackson's arrival on SCLC's staff corresponded to a new phase in the Civil Rights Movement. Jackson joined SCLC's national staff just after Congress had passed the Public Accommodations Act and the Voting

Rights Act and just as the focus in the movement for racial justice was shifting from the blatant denial of equal access provided for in the segregation laws of Southern states to the more subtle, more complex—but no less real—denials of racial justice practiced throughout American society, often popularly (but incorrectly) called "institutional racism."[15] King characterized this change in goals as the shift from freedom to equality. Having addressed the most egregious racial injustices in the legal and political arenas through the passage of the 1964 Public Accommodations Act and the 1965 Voting Rights Act, SCLC began to focus on open housing in its Chicago campaign and on the economic aspects of racial justice. SCLC's attempt to institutionalize this economic focus was epitomized in the establishment in the early 1960s of Operation Breadbasket. Breadbasket's explicit attention to some of the economic aspects of racial justice was highly controversial activity. Before this, the language of the Civil Rights Movement largely had been that of "civil rights," "equal opportunity," "desegregation," and "integration." On these topics, there had been an emerging consensus within American society that all of these were generally desirable and were in line with American ideals. But most Americans have never been comfortable with the idea of economic rights—at least not beyond the right to own property—because it seems to smack of socialism or a planned economy. This shift in the struggle for racial justice from freedom to equality (meaning equality of results, not just of opportunity)— however necessary and appropriate—was a difficult one to make in American society. It is a shift that—more than two decades later— still has not yet been agreed upon by a large segment of American society.

No one in the past twenty years has done more to advance public understanding of this shift in the struggle for racial justice than Jesse Jackson. More than any other person, he has epitomized the current phase of the struggle. This book is entitled *Beyond Opportunity* because Jackson's work over the past score of years has addressed the challenges in establishing racial justice which lie beyond enacting laws providing for equal access and opportunity—namely, achieving equity and parity in all areas of life.

Following King's view, Jackson frequently distinguishes between the Freedom Movement and the Justice Movement.[16] Before the Civil Rights Movement, Jackson argues, black people had been "locked out" of American society. Because of the successes of the Civil Rights Movement, black people were able to "move in" to many areas of American life previously closed to them. This is a "horizontal" movement and was the goal of the Freedom Movement. This is "equal opportunity." Following this horizontal movement "in," however, the goal became to "move up," to gain equality, to gain equity and parity.[17] The new goal, Jackson declares, "is to gain our share of power and responsibility in every area of American life and at every level. . . . Our sights must shift from charity to parity, from aid to trade, from social generosity to economic reciprocity, from welfare to our share."[18]

At a march in Washington, D.C., held on the twentieth anniversary of the 1963 March on Washington, Jackson assessed the changes over the previous two decades:

> Twenty years ago, we came to these hallowed grounds as a rainbow coalition to demand our freedom. Twenty years later, we have our freedom—our civil rights. . . . Apartheid is over. But, twenty years later, we still do not have equality. We have moved in. Now we must move up.
>
> Twenty years ago, we were stripped of our dignity. Twenty years later, we are stripped of our share of power. The absence of segregation is not the presence of social justice or equality.[19]

After the achievements of the Civil Rights Movement, particularly the Public Accommodations Act and the Voting Rights Act, new challenges faced those seeking racial justice. Jackson sees two very different—but highly related—kinds of challenges. The first faces black Americans. It is the challenge to take advantage of the opportunities that have become available. It is the challenge to gain equity and parity in all areas of society.[20] For black Americans, the key to this is to resist what he calls the "dependency syndrome." Self-esteem, self-motivation, and self-discipline are the principal virtues he preaches to black people because these are the keys both to taking advantage of the opportunities presently available and to enlarging these opportunities. Jackson warns black Americans not to confuse society's legal recognition of black people's civil and political rights and freedoms with the source of these rights and freedoms: "We can never be made truly free from without, and our external freedom is dependent on our changing our minds about ourselves from within."[21] As he sees it, freedom originates in the mind and in the will. Self-esteem, self-motivation, and self-discipline are the requirements if black Americans are to move beyond opportunity.

To all Americans, both black and nonblack, Jackson offers a second, related challenge which lies beyond opportunity. This is the challenge to fulfill and complete the work begun by the Civil Rights Movement. "We must continue to fight any and all institutional and structural impediments to equal . . . opportunity."[22] But now that black Americans' political and civil rights have been reaffirmed and reestablished in law, the next step in achieving racial justice is to find appropriate measures to right the wrongs that over the centuries have been committed because of race, to find ways to ensure that black Americans gain equity and parity, particularly in the economic and political arenas. "Our fundamental goal has not changed," Jackson contends. "It still is equity and parity, . . . [but] the particular target has shifted from civil (citizenship) rights to silver (economic) rights within the context of a broader human rights struggle. Increasingly, the struggle will . . . be . . . around issues that are moral, legal, political, and economic at the same time."[23]

He notes that 90 percent of the jobs paying more than $25,000 still belong to white males and concludes that this "reflects the distribution of neither genius nor merit."[24] He observes:

> Statistically, one would expect a fair employment or admissions system to produce a work force or student body reflective of the labor market or student pool available in that area. Historically, because of racism, this has not been true.[25]

Simply stopping overt discrimination has not proved sufficient to overcome the effects of more than three and a half centuries of wrongs. Ending discrimination, insofar as that has occurred, still has not resulted in black people gaining their share of power and responsibility in every area of American life and at every level. For example, Jackson estimates that, at the current rate of change, it will take nearly two more centuries to achieve equity and parity in the political arena.[26] American society must take positive steps—affirmative actions—so that black Americans can gain equity and parity. This is the challenge to all Americans that lies beyond opportunity.

SIMILARITIES TO KING

This view of America's racial situation certainly does not originate with Jesse Jackson—he simply is its most prominent contemporary black spokesperson. Martin Luther King, Jr., had a similar viewpoint, although the public mythology surrounding the establishment of his birthday as a national holiday has attempted to turn him into a man who simply dreamed about a color-blind society. An examination of his final book, *Where Do We Go from Here: Chaos or Community?* written in 1967, reveals that King, at the end of his life, had an analysis of the situation and a program for action very much like Jackson's. In this book King argued for "a radical restructuring" of American society aimed at eliminating the interrelated evils of racism, poverty, and militarism:

> Let us, therefore, not think of our movement as one that seeks to integrate the Negro into all the existing values of American history. Let us be those creative dissenters who will call our beloved nation to a higher destiny, to a new plateau of compassion, to a more noble expression of humaneness. . . . Our economy must become more person-centered than property- and profit-centered. Our government must depend more on its moral power than on its military power.[27]

In this book, King noted that, with the passage of the 1965 Voting Rights Act, the struggle for racial justice had entered a second phase, seeking equality rather than freedom and opportunity. This new phase demanded a reassessment of strategy. While it was important to break down centuries-old social and legal barriers erected to keep blacks from having equal opportunities, King believed that more fundamental changes were demanded of American society if equality and racial justice were to be achieved. Achieving equality included helping blacks "out of poverty, exploitation, or all forms of degradation."[28] King emphasized that the real cost of achieving equality lay ahead. "Jobs are harder and costlier to create than voting rolls. The eradication of slums housing millions is complex far beyond

15

integrating buses and lunch counters,"[29] but these are necessary if racial justice is to be achieved.

Yet King understood that the black-white coalition that had comprised the Civil Rights Movement was fragile and in fact was coming apart on this very idea of equality.

> The paths of Negro-white unity that had been converging crossed at Selma, and like a giant X began to diverge. Up to Selma there had been unity to eliminate barbaric conflict. Beyond it the unity had to be based on the fulfillment of equality.[30]

King also outlined the agenda of SCLC's newly formed Operation Breadbasket in *Where Do We Go from Here?* Its primary aim, he said, was to secure more and better jobs for blacks by using the economic power of black people. Boycotts and demonstrations were directed at local businesses and chain stores that did business in black communities without giving a fair share of jobs to blacks to encourage them to do so. In addition, these businesses were encouraged to deposit money in black-owned banks, to stock black-owned and -produced products, and to utilize services from black firms. The key word, King noted, was "respect." This approach says, "If you respect my dollars, you must respect my person."[31] Thus by the mid-1960s King and SCLC were turning their attention and efforts toward the economic dimensions of racism and were not simply working to break down the legal barriers to equal opportunity.

In this book, King also described how blacks should employ their newly won political power by moving into every level of political activity. His outline, written in 1967, could have served as a blueprint for Jackson's own entry into electoral politics in the mid-1980s.

> The new task of the liberation movement, therefore, is not merely to increase the Negro registration and vote; equally imperative is the development of a strong voice that is heard in the smoke-filled rooms where party debating and bargaining proceed. . . . We shall have to create leaders who embody virtues we can respect, who have moral and ethical principles we can applaud with an enthusiasm that enables us to rally support for them based on confidence and trust. . . . We shall have to master the art of political alliances. . . . They are the keys to political progress. . . . Everything Negroes need—and many of us need almost everything—will not like magic materialize from the use of the ballot. Yet as a lever of power, if it is given studious attention

and employed with the creativity we have proved through our protest activities we possess, it will help to achieve many far-reaching changes during our lifetimes. . . . The scope of struggle is still too narrow and too restricted. We must turn more of our energies and focus our creativity on the useful things that translate into power.[32]

In the final chapter of *Where Do We Go from Here?* King dealt with the role of the United States in world affairs. Because he believed that racism, poverty, and militarism are the principal problems that make stable international relations difficult, King called for a revolution of values, followed by a restructuring of national and international relationships.

Thus Martin Luther King Jr.'s understanding of the issue of racial justice at the end of his life—as expressed in 1967 in *Where Do We Go from Here?*—went far beyond the notion of "equal rights under the law" or "equal opportunity" and included political, economic, and even international dimensions of racial justice. He was clear that the Public Accommodations Act and the Voting Rights Act were simply Phase One of the struggle for racial justice; the more difficult and more costly phases lay ahead. "With Selma and the Voting Rights Act one phase of development in the civil rights revolution came to an end. A new phase opened, but few observers realized it or were prepared for its implications."[33]

CHALLENGES JACKSON FACES

Beginning his public work in this context, Jackson distinguished himself from most others advocating racial justice by articulating a stance toward social change (including racial justice) which involves a fundamental dialectic. He usually speaks of it as the dialectic between "effort" and "opportunity." While he describes it most often in addressing educational issues, this dialectic pervades all of his thinking. For black Americans, the challenge that lies beyond the achievements of the Civil Rights Movement is to take advantage of the opportunities newly available, to gain equity and parity in all areas of life. To do this, black Americans must put forth the effort to resist what Jackson calls "the dependency syndrome." "Effort must exceed opportunity for change to occur."[34] The other element of the

17

dialectic, "opportunity," refers to the institutional and policy changes which are essential to making freedom and justice first possible and then enduring. Opportunity is necessary, but it is not sufficient to establish racial justice. Thus he issues a dual challenge to Americans if this country is to go beyond the important but modest gains of the Civil Rights Movement to establish racial justice:

> We've struggled all of these years opening the doors of opportunity, and I believe in that. . . . But I've learned something else. To achieve excellence, we need more than opportunity. You can get opportunity by law, but you take advantage of opportunity by spirit and attitude. What does it matter if the doors of opportunity swing wide open but you're too drunk to stagger in? . . . So this drive to excel, to keep up, requires more than open doors. It requires the desire and the drive to be somebody.[35]

As a result of Jackson's emphasis on both effort and opportunity, he does not easily fit the standard classifications as a liberal or a conservative. Conservatives think he is on the right track as he admonishes black people to change themselves, particularly how they think about themselves, and as he advises them to use whatever political and economic resources they now possess. This side of Jackson has led some to call him a twentieth-century Booker T. Washington, admonishing his people to "cast down your buckets where you are."[36] Not surprisingly, this alienates many liberals, who wish to focus attention on the various ways American institutional arrangements have denied and continue to deny racial justice to black Americans.

On the other hand, liberals are pleased with Jackson's call for "our share" of what America has to offer; with his call for renegotiating black America's relationships with business, labor, and government; and with his vigorous defense of affirmative action, including minimum quotas, when necessary. An examination of virtually any of his speeches will show that, for all his emphasis on self-help, he also consistently calls for major institutional and policy changes in American society. He rarely emphasizes one element of the dialectic at the expense of the other. Both opportunity and effort are essential.

He is one of a new breed of civil rights leaders who focus on the new requirements of racial justice after the passage of the Public

Accommodations Act and the Voting Rights Act. These people are not addressing the problems of *establishing* the civil rights of black Americans; they presuppose their existence. Thus, in a technical sense they are more than simply "civil rights" leaders. At this point an important semantic and conceptual problem arises. Civil rights was only one part of the Civil Rights Movement; the Movement was seeking civil rights as but one step toward achieving racial justice, as will be discussed in chapter 2. The next set of issues to be addressed in the drive to achieve racial justice concerns economics and politics. The goal was for blacks to gain equity and parity in all areas of American life now that their civil and political rights had been reaffirmed and reestablished in law. As Jackson summarizes it:

> The struggle of the 1960s was never a struggle merely for civil rights. It was always a struggle for social justice. Thus the definition of the social justice movement in America in the 1980s and beyond must include a commitment to human rights, which includes: social justice (civil rights or equal protection under the law for all), economic justice (or workers' rights), and political justice (or freedom of press, of assembly, of protest, of religion, and of access to information) everywhere. Dr. King said that injustice anywhere is a threat to justice everywhere. Now we must add to that: unorganized workers anywhere are a threat to organized workers everywhere and political oppression anywhere is a threat to political freedom everywhere. And we must measure human rights everywhere by one yardstick.[37]

New issues lying beyond equal opportunity demand new strategies, or at least the adaptation of old strategies to a new set of circumstances. As will be discussed in chapter 5, the principal strategy Jackson has advocated is for black people to use whatever powers they already possess as leverage in order to create pressure for "progressive social change," which includes racial justice as its cornerstone. Black people first must change their minds about themselves. They must recognize that, rather than being impotent, they have a great deal of unused and underutilized power, most notably economic and political power. The second step involves self-motivation and self-discipline so that the powers which do exist can be developed, organized, and utilized to the utmost. Jackson reminds his audiences that "nobody will save us for us but us" and that "change does not come from the White House but from your house and my house." Only those who suffer

19

from racial injustices have a clear self-interest in ending them.[38] Third, this organized economic or political power must provide leverage to bring about change. The key term here is "leverage." While black people rarely possess a majority of the political or economic power in any particular situation, they often have enough to determine where the balance of power will lie. For example, in political contests in which the number of potential black voters exceeds the typical margin of victory, a disciplined, organized group of black voters can gain the leverage necessary to bring about changes.

The change sought by using such economic or political leverage is a "renegotiation" of the arrangement between business or labor or government and black Americans. The goal is equity and parity in all areas and on all levels. Jackson typically calls for "reciprocity," a mutually beneficial relationship, to replace exploitation, which benefits only one party in a relationship. If black voters provide a politician's margin of victory in an election, then he believes they should get a fair share of the rewards that accompany that electoral victory. This is why he calls for "our fair share" and eschews all paternalistic arrangements. As he often says: "Our sights must shift from charity to parity, from aid to trade, from social generosity to economic reciprocity, from welfare to our share."[39] The shift is from opportunity to equality.

By the late 1960s and early 1970s, Jackson, along with many others, was aware of failure of the concepts of "civil rights" and "integration" to adequately describe and define the changes that must be brought about in American society in order to achieve racial justice. "Civil rights" too often had been viewed as if it were the whole of racial justice (after all, it had been called the "Civil Rights Movement"), and "integration" too often had been used to mean that black people simply should accommodate themselves to the white mainstream in American society, to be melted in the American melting pot. Certainly the black pride and black power emphases were appropriate reactions to these. He has attempted to integrate the elements of the Civil Rights Movement with the black power movement as he sought to address the issues that lay beyond equal opportunity: equity and parity. One result is a tension in his approach between the self-help and self-reliance of black solidarity and the call for full participation of black Americans in all societal institutions. But the concept that he believes expresses the appropriate relationship between blacks, whites, and others in American society is "pluralism." He describes pluralism, however, using a variety of images, most notably the rainbow and a quilt, although he also has suggested vegetable soup as an alternative to the melting pot image.[40]

Jesse Jackson rose to national prominence just after the Civil Rights Movement had achieved its most important victories—the passage of the Public Accommodations Act and the Voting Rights Act. The civil rights coalition had been built around dismantling the Jim Crow "separate-but-equal" legal apparatus in the South and securing the civil and political rights of black Americans through new legislation. "Integration" and "equal opportunity" were the stated goals. Many in the Civil Rights Movement knew that there were many steps in the process of achieving racial justice and that the task had just begun. But few were able to articulate the next set of tasks persuasively. Even Martin Luther King, Jr.'s attempt to deal with the economic and political aspects of racial justice in his last book was not persuasive to most Americans. By the time King was assassinated in 1968, the civil rights coalition already had come apart, in part over the question of which aspects of racial justice, if any, lay beyond providing for equal opportunity.

This is the issue that Jackson has addressed in his public career, which now spans more than twenty years. In retrospect, we can see that he has faced four major problems:

1. Keeping public attention tuned to the issue of racial justice during a period of increased apathy and continued public confusion about such matters and during a period of national economic stagnation. By the time of King's assassination in 1968, few of the old allies from the days of the Civil Rights Movement remained, and the forces of racial reaction—symbolized by George Wallace's three campaigns for the Democratic party's presidential nomination—had begun to set in. In addition, changes in the national economy posed new challenges. Martin Luther King, Jr., had been working during a time of economic expansion. His proposals for dealing with poverty and the economic aspects of racial justice assumed they could be funded out of the growth in the economy and would not demand a

21

redistribution of existing resources. By the 1970s, those assumptions could not be made.

2. Defining and finding politically persuasive terms to describe the economic and political dimensions of racial justice that needed to be pursued once Jim Crow had been dismantled and equal opportunity had been established in the nation's lawbooks. It was clear that new language was called for because "civil rights," "integration," and "equal opportunity" had lost their political force and were inadequate to explain the nation's current racial problems or to point in the direction of resolution. The black power and black pride movement also pointed out some of the problems with the old formulations. Clearly, a "color-blind integration" was not going to achieve racial justice at this time in American history. New concepts and symbols were needed to capture people's imaginations and mobilize them to act.

3. Determining new strategies and tactics to pursue the new tasks confronting those pursuing racial justice. In part, different strategies were called for since black Americans had more options—but fewer allies—for achieving racial justice following the successes of the Civil Rights Movement.

4. Creating new associations or institutions to direct or assist in the quest for racial justice. The old civil rights coalition had collapsed by the time of King's assassination, and by the mid-1970s, King's old organization, SCLC, had ceased being viewed as the focus of activities for racial justice.

For the most part, Jackson has been successful in addressing all four problems. However, because there has been no national consensus about the issues of racial justice during the 1970s and 1980s, he and his work are easily misunderstood and perhaps are necessarily controversial. His attempts to face the problem of keeping the issue of racial justice before an apathetic nation have led to charges that he is seeking personal publicity, that he is an opportunist and is not a "responsible" black leader. He does attempt to make his position known through the news media and has not hesitated to rock the boat of the status quo. In addressing the problem of defining new issues, he has been portrayed as speaking to inappropriate issues or entering inappropriate areas. The assumption has been that a "civil rights leader" addresses legitimately only issues of the legal and political rights of black people, and he consistently has addressed the economic and political aspects of racism. This criticism of Jackson is loudest and can be seen most clearly when he addresses issues of American foreign policy, which is the subject of chapter 4. When facing the problem of determining new strategies, he sometimes has been charged with "reverse discrimination" because he thinks that racial consciousness and self-reliance can be positive and bases some of his strategy on it. The problem of creating new associations has proved to be the most difficult for him. Throughout his twenty years of public life he consistently has advocated coalitions as appropriate ways to seek racial justice and repeatedly has entered into coalitions. Yet he also cautions that those entering into coalitions should remain clear about their own goals and must not allow their attention to be redirected or diverted by others. Because he does not believe in organizational unity at any price, he has been branded a "maverick," someone who refuses to work with others.

All of these criticisms, while possessing an element of truth, miss the mark because they so often examine only Jackson's striking personality and style and do not seriously look at his ideas, which, more than anything else, account for his actions and positions. It is just such an examination of his ideas that follows.

2

Toward a New America

During the 1984 presidential primary campaign, Marvin Kalb of NBC News asked Jesse Jackson on "Meet the Press": "Are your priorities, deep inside yourself, . . . that of a black man who happens to be an American or the reverse?"[1] Kalb's question implied a conflict between being a black person and being a fully patriotic American. Jackson bristled at the question, said that it was inappropriate, and noted that Kalb would not think of asking it of any other candidate.

Yet, because the experience of black people in America has been so very different from that of the descendants of European immigrants—so "un-American"—raising such a question does, in fact, seem appropriate. The answer to this question, however, is not as simple as the yes or no kind of answer implied in Kalb's question; it involves a careful and critical examination of America's history.[2]

Using a description first advanced by W.E.B. DuBois in *The Souls of Black Folk* in 1903, Jackson frequently describes black Americans as " 'hyphenated Americans'—Americans, yes, but not quite." It is this "yes but not quite" approach that Jackson embodies so well and that critics such as Kalb find difficult to understand. It is a complex approach, offering both judgment and hope for America.

"AMERICA NEVER WAS AMERICA TO ME": BLACK AMERICANS AND AMERICA

As a black American, Jackson cannot gloss over some elements of American history frequently ignored by other political candidates

24

and even by historians. As he repeatedly has noted, "The history of blacks in America is unique. Blacks are the only group brought to America as slaves against their will. Other groups came as immigrants of their own free will."[3] He observes, "No other group endured 250 years of slavery and was characterized in the Constitution as three-fifths human. No other group endured 100 years of illegal apartheid, and no other group endures to this very hour the degree of daily denial, indignity, and discrimination that is heaped on black people."[4] He concludes, "Because of racism, we are in the front and bear the brunt of social and economic deterioration and in the rear of social and economic development."[5]

America, however, has never acknowledged the uniqueness of the experience of blacks in this country.[6] For example, the common view of America as a melting pot ignores both the uniqueness of each group and the fact that black Americans are never allowed to "melt," to become fully assimilated into American life. The common view of America as a land of immigrant groups ignores the crucial fact that Afro-Americans, unlike others who came voluntarily to these North American shores, came involuntarily as slaves. Jackson challenges these common views of America with his use of the rainbow, a symbol which allows each separate color to be recognized yet which forms a unity that is greater than the sum of its parts. He also claims, "America is not like a blanket, one piece of unbroken cloth—the same color, the same texture, the same size. It is more like a quilt—many patches, many pieces, many colors, many sizes, all woven and held together by a common thread."[7]

It should not have been surprising that black Americans did not choose to revel in the celebration surrounding the refurbishing of the Statue of Liberty on its one-hundredth anniversary on July 4, 1986, or the bicentennial of the Constitution in 1987. The search for liberty and freedom is not the reason black Americans came to this continent. They came against their will as slaves. Black Americans have not found this to be "one nation, under God, indivisible, with liberty and justice for all." Black Americans were not included in the "all," and black Americans have not participated in any positive aspect of American society in proportion to their numbers.

This lack of enthusiasm by blacks for national holidays celebrating American freedom is nothing new. William B. Gravely has examined the same sort of phenomenon in the first half of the nineteenth century, carefully documenting the fact that many free black Americans avoided July 4 celebrations during this period and even established alternative days to celebrate their own freedom and to call for freedom for their enslaved brothers and sisters.[8]

As Justice Thurgood Marshall, the only black person ever appointed to the Supreme Court, noted in a speech dealing with the bicentennial of the Constitution, "When the Founding Fathers used this phrase ["We the People"] in 1787, they did not have in mind the majority of America's citizens." Furthermore, it is clear that "these omissions were intentional."[9] Marshall was particularly critical of those today who simplistically seem to worship the Constitution or its framers. He observed that he did not

> find the wisdom, foresight and sense of justice exhibited by the Framers particularly profound. To the contrary, the government they devised was defective from the start, requiring several amendments, a civil war and momentous social transformation to attain the system of constitutional government, and its respect for the individual freedoms and human rights, we hold as fundamental today. . . . [If citizens] seek a sensitive understanding of the Constitution's inherent defects, and its promising evolution through 200 years of history, the celebration of the "Miracle at Philadelphia" will, in my view, be a far more meaningful and humbling experience. We will see that the true miracle was not the birth of the Constitution, but its life, a life nurtured through two turbulent centuries of our own making, and a life embodying much good fortune that was not. Thus, in this bicentennial year, we may not all participate in the festivities with flag-waving fervor. Some may more quietly commemorate the suffering, struggle and sacrifice that has triumphed over much of what was wrong with the original document, and observe the anniversary with hopes not realized and promises not fulfilled.[10]

Many black Americans, including Jackson, find their feelings about this country expressed well by words penned by Langston Hughes: "America never was America to me." Instead it is "a dream still beckoning. . . . The land that never has been yet—and yet must be."[11]

Like Hughes, Jackson views America both as a dream and as a reality. America the dream is the set of principles typically celebrated on July 4 and Thanksgiving, which Gunnar Myrdal called "the

American Creed"—the ideals "of the essential dignity of the individual human being, of the fundamental equality of all men, and of certain inalienable rights to freedom, justice, and a fair opportunity."[12] America the reality, however, has been and continues to be quite different from America the dream. For black Americans, America the reality has included Constitutionally justified slavery and segregation, followed by discrimination in all areas of life. In Jackson's approach, America the dream serves both as a standard of judgment and as a resource for transforming America the reality.

It is Jackson's willingness to freely acknowledge the negative realities of American life (on occasion, he has referred to them as a "wretched history")[13] that leads some to question his patriotism. But, as if answering the question raised by Marvin Kalb, Jackson frequently points out that black Americans have, if anything, been more patriotic than whites:

> Nobody should question any American's, but especially black America's, commitment to providing for a strong national defense. We were the first to die in the American Revolutionary War. Never in the history of the nation has any black person ever been convicted of treason. We volunteer disproportionately for the armed services and die disproportionately in military service to our country.[14]

But such patriotism by black Americans never has been fully appreciated or rewarded by the country:

> My father and his brother served in one of three all-black segregated infantries [in World War II]. Black soldiers had an especially difficult task—fighting for democracy in Europe in 1942, 1943, 1944, and 1945, without having the right to vote in America until 1965. They were inspired to fight, not for the freedom that they had, but for the freedom that they hoped for. Many of us hoped that their investment for freedom in Europe would gain freedom for us at home. These gallant men left their families in America, and all too many left their lives in Europe. Oftentimes they were used as shock troops, they had no rights at home, and they never got their Marshall Plan or reparations.[15]

Such patriotic behavior by black soldiers appears naive unless one understands this dual view of America as a reality and America as a dream. Of course, viewing life as having a contrast between reality and dreams (or between practice and ideals) is not unique to black Americans.[16] But Jackson and most black Americans employ it very differently than most white Americans. Whites typically claim that American ideals and principles currently are embodied in practice or, more frequently, that they once were. In one way or another, they often collapse the distinction between America the dream and America the reality. Thus, talk by whites about America the dream often is evidence of a nostalgic yearning for some long-ago time when they believe things were better, whereas the same kind of talk by black Americans is evidence of hope for a never-as-yet-realized promise of justice and opportunity.

Ronald Reagan's speech on July 3, 1986, celebrating the one-hundredth anniversary of the Statue of Liberty provides a striking example of the nostalgic approach:

> Some have called it mysticism or romanticism, but I've always thought that a providential hand had something to do with the founding of this country. That God had His reasons for placing this land here between two great oceans to be found by a certain kind of people. That whatever corner of the world they came from, there would be in their hearts a fervent love of freedom and a special kind of courage, the courage to uproot themselves and their families, travel great distances to a foreign shore and build there a new world of peace and freedom. . . . "The God who gave us life," Thomas Jefferson once proclaimed, "gave us liberty at the same time." But like all of God's precious gifts, liberty must never be taken for granted. . . . We are the keepers of the flame of liberty; we hold it high tonight for the world to see. . . . We dare to hope for our children that they will always find here the lady of liberty in a land that is free.[17]

This speech collapses any distinction between America the dream and America the reality, ignoring the presence in American life and history of both Native Americans and Afro-Americans, neither of whom voluntarily uprooted themselves to build a new world of peace and freedom. It also ignores the fact that many white immigrants were not welcomed by those who had arrived earlier. The Ku Klux Klan, after all, opposed the presence not only of black people; it also opposed the presence in America of Catholics and Jews.

Jackson, in the speech announcing his candidacy for the Democratic party's 1984 presidential nomination, also spoke of America the dream,[18] but, unlike Ronald Reagan, he did not imply that America the dream had ever become reality. America the dream still lay in the future. In that speech, Jackson described his quest for "a just society and a peaceful world," indicated that he hoped to "rekindle the dormant flames of idealism," and then, in words reminiscent of Langston Hughes, concluded:

This is the America that can be. This is the America that was meant to be, must be, ought to be. This is the America where all can sing with renewed pride and joy, "My country 'tis of thee. Sweet land of liberty. Of thee I sing. Land where my fathers died, land of the pilgrims' pride. From every mountaintop, let freedom ring."[19]

Thus Jackson used America the dream to provide a standard of judgment for America's present and past and to provide some basis for transforming America the reality.

RACIAL INJUSTICE AS THE STARTING POINT OF JACKSON'S ANALYSIS

Jackson's analysis of America's racial situation provides the starting point and basic frame of reference for his analysis of the rest of American society. It is difficult to understand his positions on most issues unless this fact is recognized. Because he sees all issues and areas of life as interrelated, his analysis of America's racial situation draws him into a rather full analysis of all of American life. This is what he meant when, in announcing his presidential candidacy in November of 1983, he observed: "This candidacy is not for blacks only. This is a national campaign growing out of the black experience and seen through the eyes of a black perspective—which is the perspective of the rejected."[20]

In his analysis of America's racial situation, Jackson points out that—as a result of this country's 350-year history of slavery, segregation, and discrimination—black Americans find themselves behind in nearly every area of American life that is desirable and ahead in nearly every area that is undesirable. For example, black unemployment consistently is twice that for whites; life expectancy is several years fewer for blacks; black family income is less than 60 percent of that for whites; and school drop-out rates are higher. Jackson frequently illustrates his point by citing statistics such as these:

There is 1 white attorney for every 680 whites, 1 black attorney for every 4,000 blacks; 1 white physician for every 649 whites, 1 black physician for every 5,000 blacks; 1 white dentist for every 1,900 whites, 1 black dentist for every 8,400 blacks. Less than 1 percent of all engineers are black. Blacks make up less than 1 percent of all practicing chemists.[21]

These gaps exist, Jackson claims, "not because of nature, genes, or market forces, but because of the historic and lingering legacy of racism and discrimination."[22]

He vigorously disagrees with those, such as William Julius Wilson, author of *The Declining Significance of Race*,[23] who believe that class, rather than race, is the fundamental negative reality confronting black Americans. Jackson declares:

> As an oppressed people, we share with others a common economic plight—we are part of a despised, rejected, oppressed, and exploited economic class. In addition, however, we alone bear another, and more fundamental, yoke around our collective neck. We are also a member of a racial caste, the black caste. . . . Being a black American in white America is to be victimized by both class and caste, but for us caste must be seen as central to our predicament.
>
> All black Americans—Ph.D.'s and No D's—got the right to sit in the front of the bus on the same day. All black Americans—whatever our class—got the right to use public accommodations on the same day. All black Americans—regardless of our pedigree—got the right to vote on the same day. We make some distinctions among ourselves—poor, middle class, upper class; urban and rural; Republican, Democrat, or Independent—but our most fundamental distinction is caste. We suffer from caste rejection. That is the fundamental status of black America.[24]

The early assessments of Jackson's 1988 campaign for the Democratic party's nomination for president bear out his basic contention. Although he became the front-runner in the polls following Gary Hart's withdrawal from the race, this fact never was taken seriously. Roger Simon's comments are instructive: "The polls do not matter in the case of Jesse Jackson, we are told, because Jesse Jackson cannot become president of the United States. Why? . . . Could it be that Jesse Jackson can be eliminated from serious thought because he is black? Ah, I think we have hit on it."[25]

In Jackson's view, racism is the belief that some people are superior and others inferior as a result of their race. "Racism is fundamentally a moral problem, a problem of human values, running from our minds to our local communities and to our international community."[26] On the most fundamental level, racism is "a disease of the soul,"[27] a kind of "social cancer."[28] Like cancer, once racism comes near the heart, it spreads all over the body.[29] He continually asserts that racism is scientifically untrue, theologically immoral, psychologically unhealthy, and economically and politically unfeasible.[30] These are the major levels of the problem of racism that he addresses.

On the theological level, racism maintains, contrary to Judeo-Christian principles, that not all human beings are created in the image of God (see Gen. 1:26). The foundation of Jackson's view of human beings is his belief that all people—without regard to race, gender, or economic status—are children of God. That is why he declares "I am somebody." Everyone is somebody because all are God's children. Tragically, however, the Christian churches typically have propounded rather than attacked racism, they have been part of the problem rather than part of the solution.[31]

The psychological distortion that results from racism is twofold. It unduly puffs up the self-importance of the group thought to be racially superior, while at the same time it leads to unnecessary and destructive negative self-images among those thought to be racially inferior. While Jackson occasionally addresses the first problem, most of the focus in his inspirational and motivational speeches is on the destructive negative self-images held by many black people.

His chant, with which he opens most student rallies and the weekly Saturday morning forums at Operation PUSH, deals with both the theological and psychological dimensions of racism.

> I am somebody.
> I may be poor,
>   but I am somebody.
> I may be uneducated,
> I may be unskilled,
>   but I am somebody.
> I may be on welfare,
> I may be prematurely pregnant,
> I may be on drugs,
> I may be victimized by racism,
>   but I am somebody.
> Respect me. Protect me. Never neglect me.
> I am God's child.

SCLC's Operation Breadbasket and later Jackson's own Operation PUSH were explicitly designed to deal with the economic dimensions of racism. Examining the political dimensions of racism, he observes that politicians have used race (and also gender and class) to divide voters.

> Racism has divided families, communities, nations, and our concept of justice. Racism has split religious institutions and distorts the image of God. Racism has allowed politicians to exploit our emotions for their short-term political gain but at a long-term loss to their constituencies, their nations, and the world.[32]

American racism, however, affects not only black Americans but the entire nation as well. Jackson believes that racism is the number-one threat to domestic tranquility[33] and is the principal obstacle to creating a new world order characterized by peace and justice. "But be clear, blacks alone are not the victims. We are simply the weathervane signaling what is just ahead for the rest of the society. We are simply the first to 'get wind' of what is going on in the society as a whole."[34] Racism obscures Americans' view of the important problems facing them as a people. They allow themselves to be sidetracked by racial considerations and to waste their energies fighting over race when they should be debating public policy. Racism has "split our [national] psyche and has forced us to pay the economic and moral burden of two societies."[35] "Racism has blinded Europe, North America, and most of the 'white Western world,' and has left moral cataracts and scar tissue on our world eyes. Thus our vision of a new world order is blurred, unclear, and racist."[36] The United States, which has 4 percent of the world's people, "cannot afford racial polarization. We cannot afford to waste our time arguing about transportation to school rather than edification at school. . . . We must begin to choose reason over race and see race and racism as a fundamental threat to the character of our nation."[37]

Jackson often talks about "removing the cataracts of race" because they keep Americans from seeing the true nature of many political and economic issues and from seeing the interrelationship among so many of them. In a speech before a joint session of the Alabama legislature, for example, he argued that Americans are wasting their energies fighting over school desegregation when they should be dealing with economic policy:

Too often, however, we have focused on the minor and lost sight of the major. We have put too much of our focus on the schoolyard and lost sight of the shipyard. Integration in the schoolyard *does not* threaten America—in fact it will help us—but unfair trade and slave-labor competition in the shipyard *does* threaten us.[38]

He argues that Americans should "leave . . . racial battlegrounds, come to economic common ground, and rise to moral higher ground."[39]

Because racism obscures the interconnected nature of reality, it makes people view problems as isolated from one another and keeps citizens isolated from one another. The interrelationship between issues which is obscured by racism provides the basis for the program of Jackson's Rainbow Coalition. For example, in speaking of the Reagan administration's foreign policy, which Jackson called one of "injustice, inhumanity, and intimidation,"[40] he pointed out the " 'deadly connection' between conventional wars abroad, nuclear weapons escalation and threats, deteriorating living standards at home, and blatant support for racism."[41]

> We must see these issues in their interrelatedness rather than their separateness. The idea that these problems are separate, unrelated, and far-removed from us is an illusion. What's more, these problems are rooted in the institutional racism here at home.[42]

People who can see what is in their true economic and political interest rather than having their vision clouded by the cataracts of race are potential members of Jackson's Rainbow Coalition.

Because racism has become so insinuated in American life during the past 350 years, combatting racism means addressing a whole host of problems in American life. Jackson gave a glimpse of the range of these problems when he assessed the state of black Americans midway through the Reagan administration's time in office. He concluded:

> The economic, political, and social state of black America is not new. Its state or condition has only been intensified. Black America is in an intensified state of brokenness, misery, and despair. . . .
> Black America is being victimized by a cutback in schools and an increase in jails; a cutback in food stamps and an increase in hunger and malnutrition; a cutback in affirmative action and an increase in unemployment; a cutback in health care and an increase in infant

mortality; a cutback in housing and an increase in home foreclosures and in people living in their cars; a cutback in legal enforcement and an increase in racial discrimination.

We are used for scapegoats—as the cause of the nation's misery—and we are the objects of violent attacks by the KKK, the Nazis, the police, and the government—sometimes they are one and the same.[43]

In this assessment, he sees schools, jails, food stamps, hunger, unemployment, health care, housing, law enforcement, and racial discrimination as problems that must be addressed if racial justice is to be achieved in American society.

While Jackson identifies racism as the primary negative principle in American life, he also identifies several other negative principles: greed, both corporate and individual; a rugged individualism which leads to both narcissism and a self-righteous callousness toward the needs of the poor and the rejected; American arrogance toward other nations, particularly those in the Third World; reliance on military power for national security; and glorification of violence and reliance on force in solving problems.[44] These negative principles, like the positive principles of America the dream, have come to characterize much that is "American." Thus "America" is a symbol that stands for many things, some of them positive and some negative.

The second, negative set of principles not only causes problems in American society and around the world, but it also blinds Americans from seeing these problems clearly. For example, Jackson concludes that corporate greed has weakened America's principal industries,[45] and individual greed has brought short-term gain to a few but long-term pain for many and for the country.[46] Rugged individualism has blinded many Americans to the problems in American society, causing them to "blame the victim."[47] Americans' typical attitude that everything they do is better than anyone else, that America is or must be "number one," blinds them to the interconnected nature of the world community in the last part of the twentieth century, to America's dependence on the rest of the world. Jackson believes that militarism and the glorification of violence blind Americans to the truths that military power ultimately rests upon moral power and that security ultimately depends upon just relationships as much as upon arsenals full of weapons.

Thus he believes that America—rather than having a single set of consistent principles—is "full of contradictions and inconsistencies."[48] As he noted in a 1984 campaign speech in Mexico City:

> The United States is the mining of the harbors of Nicaragua, but it is also the Rainbow Coalition. The United States is the support of racist and repressive regimes in South Africa and El Salvador, but it is also the civil rights struggle of Martin Luther King, Jr. The United States is support for the hated Somoza contras in Honduras and Costa Rica, but it is also 10,000 Mexican Americans, blacks, and progressive whites marching in Los Angeles last week to stop the repressive Simpson-Mazzoli immigration control bill. The United States is budget deficits and their corollary of higher interest rates, but it is also the young Americans here tonight on their way to Nicaragua.[49]

The prominence—even celebration—of these negative principles in contemporary American life has led to what Jackson calls "a civilizational crisis." This crisis has both personal and societal dimensions. He sees the personal dimension in such things as alcohol and drug abuse; engaging in sex without love, making unwanted babies; violence; suicide; and the loss of hope. He sees evidence of the societal or structural dimension in America's sexism, militarism, racism, and economic exploitation.[50] He provided perhaps his most inclusive description of this civilizational crisis during the speech announcing his candidacy for the Democratic party's 1984 presidential nomination:

> As I look out over the landscape of America and see 10 million able-bodied men and women who are actively seeking employment but unable to find jobs; as I read with sorrow about the record number of foreclosures on homes and farms because people who have worked all their lives are unable to make the mortgage notes; as I behold families sleeping in automobiles and under bridges and standing numbly and shamefully in cheese lines because they have no food in the wealthiest nation on earth; as I see schools being closed and jails being built, teachers being fired and jailers being hired; as I watch our national tax code become increasingly regressive, unfair, and full of wasteful, unjustifiable subsidies for big corporations and wealthy individuals; as I watch the leaders of the nation's largest corporations use windfall tax breaks for foreign investment, conglomerate mergers, acquisitions, and other fast-buck schemes which add nothing to our national levels of employment, productivity, or output; as I witness students cry because educational opportunity grants and loans are no

35

longer available to enable them to attend college; as I watch the distress of senior citizens who are terrified because they fear their Social Security benefits will be taken from them; as I watch our government join forces with undemocratic, oppressive regimes in South Africa, the Philippines, and El Salvador and see our flag burned by nations because we are thought to be a contradiction of the freedom we proclaim; as I watch American soldiers die needlessly on foreign battlefields in undeclared wars without clear missions; as I observe our unfair immigration policies and watch our Mexican neighbors being met at our borders by armed guards and Haitian refugees locked up in concentration camps while our Canadian neighbors and refugees from Poland and the Soviet Union are greeted with open arms and resettlement assistance; as I witness astronomical increases in poverty, unemployment, and preventable disease on Indian reservations and witness the reckless use of the powers of our government to usurp land and other national resources that rightfully belong to Native Americans; as I witness increasing discrimination against people because of their sexual preferences; and as I watch our Department of Justice refuse to enforce civil rights laws, aggressively oppose civil rights laws, and lead the effort to dismantle federal civil rights enforcement machinery—it is clear to me that if America stands before the mirror of justice it must answer Ronald Reagan's question [of 1980] "Are you better off today than you were four years ago?" with a resounding "NO!"[51]

This civilizational crisis is a moral crisis, a crisis in fundamental priorities. In his campaign in 1984, Jackson called for both America and individual Americans to go "a new way." This new way is a kind of individual and social conversion. As he noted, "Conversion means a change of heart. That's what America needs—conversion from a despairing society to a caring society."[52]

He calls on Americans to care for "the basic needs of the people of America and the world."[53] He takes his cue from the Preamble to the U.S. Constitution: "We the people of the United States, in order to form a more perfect union, establish justice, insure domestic tranquility, provide for the common defence, promote the general welfare, and secure the blessings of liberty to ourselves and our posterity, do ordain and establish this Constitution for the United States of America." He looks at these positive purposes of government and calls for an "active, caring government"[54] rather than for a minimalist or laissez-faire one. "We must do more than survive; we must build a civilization on the principles of peace, justice, and mutual respect."[55]

In fact, he argues that, if government is to pay special attention to any one group, it should be the dispossessed and the rejected, not the rich and powerful. "We must look at every aspect of United States . . . policy that has favored the rich over the poor, the few over the many."[56] Ensuring that their basic life needs are met will contribute to everyone's welfare, unlike the benefits that come from favoring the rich and powerful.

But, as Jackson views American society, he concludes that the second, negative set of principles increasingly has come to dominate American life, both at home and abroad. Consequently, Americans have difficulty even recognizing that many important social problems exist, much less mobilizing the resources necessary to address them.

RELIGIOUS AND POLITICAL RESOURCES FOR SOCIAL TRANSFORMATION

How can Americans find a way out of their civilizational crisis? In his analysis of American society, Jackson concludes: "At the center of every political, economic, legal, and social issue is the spiritual, moral, and ethical dimension."[57] Thus he seeks to find some common religious, moral, and ethical principles to guide a pluralistic American society seeking to find its way. He identifies three main sources for these public principles: (1) the positive American values of the American creed, America the dream; (2) the religious traditions of Judaism and Christianity, traditions shared in some way by most Americans; and (3) the general lessons of history, a kind of natural law.

He challenges America and individual Americans to live up to their highest values: "give me your tired, your poor, your huddled masses," . . . "with liberty and justice for all," . . . "life, liberty, and the pursuit of happiness." But, while America the dream is an important source for social criticism and for a vision of the way things could be, he clearly recognizes its limitations, particularly as it has affected black Americans. Quoting Langston Hughes, Jackson

37

pointedly observes: "America never was America to me."[58] The traditional American ideals have never been fully applied to black Americans.

Jackson often turns to the prophetic tradition within Judaism (and to its later incorporation into Christianity) when seeking moral and religious principles. He particularly likes to quote the passage from Isaiah which Jesus read in the synagogue upon beginning his public ministry, claiming that this is the proper measure of America: "The Spirit of the Lord God is upon me, because the Lord has anointed me to bring good tidings to the afflicted; he has sent me to bind up the brokenhearted, to proclaim liberty to the captives, and the opening of the prison to those who are bound; to proclaim the year of the Lord's favor."[59] In addition, he frequently quotes Jesus, who, when indicating which people finally will find favor with God, said, "inasmuch as ye have done it unto one of the least of these my brethren, ye have done it unto me."[60] He argues that the proper measure of national greatness is "how we treat the least of these: young people in the dawn of life, old people in the sunset of life, and poor people in the pit of life."[61]

His affirmation of Christian and Jewish values does not, however, constitute an attempt to embody parochial religious positions and principles in American public policy. He does not attempt to identify what is distinctive about Christianity as it approaches public policy issues but instead attempts to identify what it holds in common with other major religious traditions, such as Judaism and Islam. Jackson believes that no group—be they Christian ministers, Jewish rabbis, or American politicians—has special access to these Judeo-Christian principles. These are to be public, not private, principles. He never claims that Christian doctrine provides clear, specific guidance in specific public policy choices. Religious commitments do not obviate the need for careful social analysis and the need to make choices among various policies and the strategies for achieving them. Rather, religious commitments provide only general guidance and general principles as choices are made.

He finds a third source of criticism and transformation in "the lessons of history." These are truths that can be learned by examining history carefully and critically, a kind of natural law. While he finds them affirmed in the religious traditions of Judaism, Christianity, and Islam, he believes that they are available to everyone, regardless of religious or political affiliation. Among these things that will prove to be true in the long run are: although the arc of the universe is long, it bends toward justice;[62] right is might, not vice versa;[63] those who side with the few at the expense of the many will lose;[64] and repression can only delay—not defeat—the liberation of oppressed people.[65] In a similar vein, particularly in foreign policy issues, he reminds Americans of the importance of being on the "right side" of history.[66] If not, "the wheels of history will grind our arrogance down to pulp."[67]

These three sources of social criticism are all ways he has tried to identify public, rather than private, principles for social action. These are three different ways of trying to understand and explain the nature of reality itself. He sees them as complementary and overlapping approaches, rather than as distinctive. Taken together, these three sources can provide some general, agreed-upon bases for judging America the reality and for transforming it. The fact that he views America the dream and Judeo-Christian principles in this way accounts in part for his use of religious language to talk about political matters.

His co-mingling of religious and political issues in this country which boasts of having successfully built "a wall of separation between church and state"[68] not surprisingly makes many people—including many of his political supporters—nervous. It may be worthwhile to be reminded of the perspective of the black church, namely, that the *political* act of resisting racism is done for a religious reason (to affirm one's own self-worth) as well as for political ones (to advance one's own self-interest, to promote a more inclusive and just society, etc.). Since all acts of resistance to racism have this dual religious-political character, it should not be surprising that the language used to describe them is both religious and political.

But this co-mingling of religious and political language and imagery in American politics certainly is not limited to black Americans seeking racial justice or to Jackson's political campaigning. In his landmark essay in 1967, "Civil Religion in America," Robert Bellah noted that God has been "mentioned or referred to in all [presidential]

39

inaugural addresses but Washington's second, which is a very brief (two paragraphs) and perfunctory acknowledgement."[69] But the issue is more than language. Herbert Richardson, for example, has noted that "Americans talk and act as if the *ultimate* questions of human life were being decided in the realm of the *polis;* and Americans also believe that political categories have a special appropriateness for symbolizing ultimate reality and man's fulfillment."[70] Bellah noted that the idea that there is "the obligation, both collective and individual, to carry out God's will on earth" is "a theme that lies very deep in the American tradition."[71] This recognition of the religious character of many ideas about America helps account for the power and persistence in American life of such notions as Manifest Destiny. For many Americans, America is not only a geographical location, it is an idea, a dream with a religious character.

Successful public leaders have understood this. Ronald Reagan is one who has made good use of this religious aspect of America the dream in his speeches. Following the deaths of the crew members on space shuttle Challenger in January of 1986, for example, Reagan spoke of these seven men and women as pioneering American heroes who voluntarily sacrificed themselves for our sake. Their deaths, he claimed, show that greatness and meaning lie in adventure and discovery, in taking risks and pushing into the future.

Jackson also understands this well. In 1984, he argued that, in order for the Democrats to defeat Reagan, it was not enough to be anti-Reagan. They had to offer a "superior vision":

> Reagan has offered the American people a coherent vision, an ideology based on fighting communism and promoting the growth of American corporations around the world. We must offer an equally coherent vision based on fighting poverty, disease, and oppression and promoting economic development that meets the needs of people around the world.
>
> Reagan seeks to build the MX. We must seek to rebuild America's cities. Reagan would invest in an ever escalating defense budget. We must invest in the minds of our children. Reagan offers the nation Star Wars. We must offer the nation an urban policy, an educational policy that will save the youth in our cities, who now walk the streets with no hope for the future. Reagan offers to turn our national resources over to the highest bidder. We must seek to preserve them for our children and our children's children. Reagan would sacrifice the welfare of the many to the short-term economic interests of the

elite few. We must set our nation on a course where the full spiritual, moral, and physical resources of our people can be realized. Reagan offers a vision of a world at war. We must offer a vision of peace and justice.[72]

Jackson understands that politics, at the most important level, deals with choosing which of several competing views of reality and the future will be embodied in public policies. This is the meaning of his statement, "at the center of every political, economic, legal, and social issue is the spiritual, moral, and ethical dimension."[73] The questions for politics are, first, which vision to act upon and, second, which steps should be taken to embody that vision.

PROGRESSIVE POLITICS

Jackson's call for a new America often means to change America the reality so that it is more like America the dream. Once public principles have been agreed upon, they must be implemented. Often this means taking principles already held to be valid for some groups and extending them to others. For example, the main theme in his 1984 campaign was that all Americans—regardless of their race, their sex, their class, or any other characteristic—have a right to enjoy a fair share of the benefits that this country has to offer. He agrees with Thurgood Marshall's observation, quoted earlier in this chapter, "when the Founding Fathers used this phrase ["We the People"] in 1787, they did not have in mind the majority of America's citizens."[74] But Jackson argues that the positive set of American principles must be extended to all Americans. "Life, liberty, and the pursuit of happiness. That is the American dream. Farmworkers deserve their share in that dream. So do farmers."[75] He believes that government must secure the political and civil rights of all citizens. Then government needs to be concerned about the needs of all of its people.

Sometimes he argues for extending agreed-upon principles to new issues. For example, he calls for extending American democratic principles into the realm of foreign policy, where, since World War II, he believes the United States has moved from asserting traditional American democratic ideals to a more "realistic" stance. He recalls: "Before America had power, America had values that made America

41

the hope of the free world."[76] Accordingly, "America must return to being a force for peace, for democracy, for human decency. A beacon of hope, not a helicopter gunship of despair."[77] "We need to devise a new strategy . . . that takes into account our historic heritage—our anticolonial origins, our multinational population, rich in the cultures of all the peoples of the world, our internal struggles for social, economic reform, and justice."[78] In short, he argues that "we must have a foreign policy that is not foreign to American values."[79]

The same holds true for policies regarding the poor and powerless. Here, he calls for an active, caring government that is primarily concerned with the common good, not simply with protecting the rights of those who already have power and wealth to get more: "Measure America's greatness by how far she reaches out and reaches back. 'Give me your tired, your poor, your huddled masses'—that's what made America great."[80]

In extending what he calls "American values" into new areas of American life or to new groups, such as the poor and the powerless, he is calling for more than piecemeal reforms. He recognizes that he is calling for a new America, a transformed America. In a new America, national greatness would be measured in moral rather than economic or military terms: "The new standard for measuring America's greatness must be how we treat children in the dawn of life; how we treat poor people in the pit of life; and how we treat old people in the sunset of life."[81]

Because there are two sets of American principles, one positive, the other negative, American principles cannot be the final measure of things. Consequently, Jackson characterizes himself as neither a "liberal" nor a "conservative" but as a "progressive" and claims that black Americans typically are progressive.

> Black America has always been on the cutting edge of progressive politics in America. We are not conservative, nor are we liberals. We are progressives. We don't seek to keep things as they are [as conservatives do] or to modify things as they are [as liberals do]. We seek to change our nation. We don't want cruel slavery or modified slavery, we want freedom—no slavery at all.[82]

Just as he does not collapse the distinction between America the dream and America the reality, neither does he collapse the distinction between individual conversion and social action. This dual emphasis on conversion, which usually is characterized as "conservative," and on social action, which usually is characterized as "liberal" or "radical," while not unusual among black Americans, particularly black Christians, rarely exists among white Americans and thus often befuddles political analysts, who tend not to know the realities of black America. For example, Jackson asserted:

> Our campaign is a moral and political crusade to transform the quality of American life. We want to restore a moral quality to the political decisions that affect our lives at home and the decisions that affect the lives of our brothers and sisters around the globe. We want to set our nation on a course where the full spiritual, moral, and physical resources of our people can be realized. We want to end the exploitation and oppression of the many by the few.[83]

The first two sentences, which emphasize conversion and moral values, could have been spoken by Jerry Falwell or Pat Robertson. But Jackson's social analysis from the point of view of the disinherited, seen in the last sentence, sets him apart both from white conservative religious leaders in politics and from conventional political liberals. Thus his preference for the term "progressive."

In retrospect, then, Jackson's answer to Marvin Kalb's question on "Meet the Press" ("Are you . . . a black man who happens to be an American or the reverse?") should have been that he understood himself to be a black American Christian who, in the final analysis, is a citizen of the world. Being black, being American, and being Christian all give him particular angles of vision on reality and on the appropriate direction for social change. However, each of these particularistic angles of vision finally must be judged and adjusted by the others. This is what he means when he talks about "the lessons of history" or suggests that things be held up to "the mirror of justice." The moral and religious principles that lie at the heart of every political, economic, legal, and social issue and that point the way toward a new America are to be inclusive and universal, not private and exclusive; they should be the result of public debate, not a substitute for it. In his view, America has not yet been fully constructed. "Those who would build this national house, . . . and make a difference in the world, must build on the solid foundations of truth, justice, mercy, peace, equality, and freedom."[84]

3

Humane Priorities at Home: Reconceiving U.S. Domestic Policies

What is the substance of this "new America" that Jackson seeks? The theme of his 1984 presidential campaign was "Jobs, Peace, and Justice," and this capsulizes his general approach to all public policy issues. It recognizes the interrelation among various issues; it recognizes the primary importance of economic, human rights, and world peace issues; and it recognizes the interdependence of foreign and domestic issues. He argues for creating a new America along the lines suggested in the previous chapter: an America whose national greatness is measured not by the size of her gross national product or her nuclear stockpiles but "by how far she reaches out and reaches back,"[1] an America concerned about jobs, peace, and justice.

"Invest in America" is the theme of his 1988 campaign. Like his earlier campaign's theme, it recognizes the interdependence of various issues and areas of life and of the various groups of people in America. It also recognizes the importance of hope and vision when addressing public policy issues. We "must not only have the courage and the conscience to expose the slummy side [of American life]. We must have the conviction and vision to show America the sunny side, the way out."[2] Here again Jackson employs the dialectic between America the reality and America the dream, discussed in chapter 2. The "invest in America" theme also indicates his belief that it is both better and cheaper in the long run to avoid or solve social problems in advance—to develop America and her people—rather than to try to pick up the pieces after they fall apart. "Education and employment cost less than ignorance and incarceration."[3] "We must put America back to work because it costs less to employ our people—making them productive and giving them dignity—than it does to pay for unemployment compensation, welfare, and the personal and social destruction that comes from a hopeless, downtrodden, and unemployed people."[4]

For a more detailed understanding of his view of domestic political issues, it is helpful to examine his analysis of four issues: black economic development, education, poverty, and hunger.

BLACK ECONOMIC DEVELOPMENT

In July of 1981, Jackson's Operation PUSH launched a nationwide "withdrawal of enthusiasm" campaign against Coca-Cola with the slogan, "Don't Choke on Coke." This followed nearly a year of on-again, off-again negotiations between Operation PUSH and Coca-Cola to secure better economic relationships between Coca-Cola and black Americans. Coca-Cola finally agreed to sign a "moral covenant," pledging to name black people to its board of directors; to make wholesale distributorships and bottling franchises available to black people; to do more business with black-owned banks, media, and advertising agencies; and to increase the percentage of blacks in both white- and blue-collar positions with the company. Critics charged that Jackson had "blackmailed" Coke and that Coca-Cola had "knuckled under."[5]

Was this just another example of Jesse Jackson being a "publicity hound," as some have charged?[6] To be sure, he rarely shuns the publicity connected with any of his activities. But the campaign against Coca-Cola was not an isolated activity designed to gain personal publicity for him; rather, it was one instance in a long line of activities over two decades designed to secure economic development for black Americans.

The initial purpose of the Southern Christian Leadership Conference's Operation Breadbasket, headed by Jackson, was to deal with some of the economic dimensions of racial justice. Accordingly, much of Operation Breadbasket's (and later Operation PUSH's) attention was directed toward black economic development. During the late 1960s and early 1970s, most of the activity was local. Breadbasket attempted to put pressure on white-owned and -run stores operating in black neighborhoods to employ black people, to do business with black businesses, and to end practices which exploited black consumers (such as chain grocery stores charging higher prices for goods that were inferior to those found in their suburban stores). Boycotts of offending stores were organized, and some "moral covenants" were signed. These moral covenants typically included pledges by firms not only to hire black people to work in their stores but also to deposit some of their money in black banks and to use the services of black legal firms, advertising agencies, and scavenger companies. This was an attempt to build some stable economic institutions which then could become the foundation for a stable community.

During the first half of the 1980s Operation PUSH used these same tactics but directed them at national companies rather than just at Chicago businesses. Moral covenants were signed with, among others, Coca-Cola, Seven-Up, Kentucky Fried Chicken, Burger King, Avon, General Foods, Quaker Oats, Miller, and Budweiser. Together these moral covenants involved agreements to return more than $2.5 billion annually to the black community.[7]

The underlying theme of Jackson's activities in the economic arena over the past two decades has been that black Americans need to "renegotiate" their relationship with white corporate America based on two standards: equity and reciprocity. Equity, which he refers to as "our share," is the distribution of such things as power, responsibility, and opportunity without regard to race. The gap between black and white Americans in these things exists, he argues, "not because of nature, genes, or market forces, but because of . . . racism."[8] "Black Americans do not lack capability, they lack opportunity. . . . The basic problem black Americans have with the exclusively private business approach to solving our economic woes is its policy of racial exclusion."[9] Because of this, he argues that equity demands a sharing of power, responsibility, and opportunity among groups in rough proportion to their presence in a given institution or population. Thus in a community with a labor pool

46

that is 30 percent black, he argues that 30 percent of a store's employees should be black. That is what he calls "our share."

By reciprocity, he refers to "a fair return on investment."[10] If black consumers "invest" money in companies by purchasing their goods or by shopping at their stores, thereby keeping them in business or giving them a profit, they should receive a fair return on that investment. Their contribution or investment should be acknowledged and rewarded, resulting in a reciprocal relationship. A reciprocal relationship may not be a relationship among equals, but it is one in which both parties recognize their dependence upon the other. It involves mutual respect rather than exploitation. In this way, Jackson's drive toward racial justice goes beyond providing for equality of opportunity. It fosters a new America built upon a vision of jobs, peace, and justice for all.

But investing in this new America requires a reconceiving of many domestic policies. He notes that corporate America long has acknowledged the presence of black America, but it has defined it as a "special market." In this way it relates to black Americans "as essentially consumers and workers, but never as co-partners in development, production, ownership, and shared wealth. Black America is always defined on the demand side of the economic ledger, never on the supply side."[11] This is the relationship that he seeks to renegotiate.

Often the situation has been similar to the one Jackson and his associates found in 1980 and 1981 when they examined the Coca-Cola Company's practices. While blacks constituted about 14 percent of Coke's total domestic business (which included much more than soft drinks), and while black per-capita consumption of soft drinks was three times that of white, Coca-Cola did not have a single black person on its board of directors. It had almost five hundred bottling franchises and nearly four thousand wholesale distributorships, yet not one was black-owned. Coca-Cola spent $343 million in 1979 on advertising, yet less than half of 1 percent was spent with black advertising firms. Only recently had Coke begun to advertise in black newspapers and magazines and on black radio stations. Jackson concluded that Coca-Cola did not do "the amount of business" with black banks, savings and loan companies, and insurance companies or make use of black physicians, lawyers, and accountants "that the large investment of black consumer dollars in Coca-Cola would call for."[12]

Because blacks had not secured a proportion of jobs and business with Coca-Cola comparable to the black proportion of the labor pool, Coca-Cola, Jackson claimed, had violated the principle of equity. Because Coca-Cola did not do business with the black community in proportion to the black share of Coca-Cola's sales, it had violated the principle of reciprocity. Thus this relationship lacked mutual respect. Accordingly, he sought to renegotiate it, and in 1981 Coca-Cola signed a moral covenant with Operation PUSH. Among other things, Coca-Cola agreed to appoint thirty-two black wholesalers within the year, to lend $1.5 million to black entrepreneurs entering the beverage industry, and to name a black member to its board of directors (it named former U.N. Ambassador Donald F. McHenry).

Central to Jackson's notion of reciprocity is self-respect. Without self-respect, there is little likelihood of mutual respect, and self-respect, he maintains, is essential in initiating any change. Without self-respect, people do not understand the power they may have. Without self-respect, relationships of dependency and exploitation can continue to exist indefinitely.

With self-respect, however, change is possible. As he reminds black people, "If our attitudes are inclined toward freedom and if our minds are committed to it, then social, economic, and political freedom will be the byproduct. . . . Even within the chains of limited economic and political options, we are not impotent."[13] Among the powers black people potentially have in the late 1980s are nearly twenty million votes and more than $200 billion in disposable personal income. As Jackson likes to put it: economically, this makes black America "the ninth-richest 'nation' in the world." In addition, black America "does more business with corporate America than Russia, China, and several other nations combined. Politically, its . . . eligible voters are more people than the world's Jewish population."[14] But such potential power must be developed and organized in order to become effective, in order for black America to be able to renegotiate the current arrangement with white corporate America.

The goals of such renegotiations are self-reliance and development. Jackson argues that, although the concept of self-reliance is "fundamentally an economic and political one, it also involves a spiritual and psychological aspect as well—a shift from expectations of dependence to expectations of self-reliance and self-determination."[15] The concept of self-reliance functions in two complementary ways for him. In his view, this shift of expectations from dependence to self-reliance must occur in black people as the first step in bringing about any social change. The dependency syndrome must be shattered. But self-reliance is more than a precondition for social change; it also is one of its goals. Self-reliance as a goal refers to relationships characterized by mutuality or reciprocity rather than dependency. As he puts it, black and oppressed people need "economic reciprocity" not "social generosity," "trade" not "aid."[16]

But oppressed and disinherited people do not become fully self-reliant in the economic arena simply by declaring themselves to be so. Development is necessary. The first step, of course, is for black people to marshal and organize whatever resources and powers they already may have. These resources and powers must then be employed in disciplined ways to gain "their share." What is gained, however, must be reinvested in the black community in ways that help those communities develop. The goal must be more than employment for a few black people—or even for all black people—because "jobs are not enough. Full employment with no pay is slavery, and employment without ownership is colonialism."[17] Community building and economic development—not private profit—are the goals. For example, one of Jackson's criticisms of Lyndon Johnson's "Great Society" programs of the 1960s is that they did not adequately address the issue of black institutional development:

> Poverty money was put in downtown white banks, not in black banks. Insurance was taken out with white insurance companies, seldom with black insurance companies. Advertising was done in the white media, but only sprinkled in the black media. White construction firms that hired blacks did the building, not black construction firms.[18]

Because the world is interrelated, however, self-reliance and development of the black community can be no more than proximate goals. Ultimately, the goal of renegotiating black America's relationship with white America is the full development of black America so that *all*—not only black people—can gain.[19] This is the movement beyond freedom, beyond opportunity, to justice.

What black America has always understood, but what the rest of America has seldom understood, is that progress for us means progress for all Americans. But progress for some of America is not necessarily progress for all of America. Rising tides don't lift all boats, especially those boats stuck at the bottom. But when boats at the bottom move, all boats move. . . . [I want] to interpret to the rest of America how a progressive coalition which includes blacks as an integral part of the coalition will benefit the entire nation—i.e., how jobs, peace, and justice will make America more just, more humane, and more secure at the same time.[20]

Jackson usually argues that black Americans are being frozen or locked-out of full participation in corporate life and stresses the positive benefits that will come to all Americans from the economic development of black America. As he examined the situation in 1982, he observed:

If you think the baseball lock-out of Jackie Robinson was immoral and foolish, the industrial lock-out and rejection of the black American economic market and its potential for development is absolute economic nonsense. We have ideas, energy, and money to invest and risk. . . . The black American economy is an unexplored treasure chest in a wrecked ship that now must be opened, inspected, and liberated. What does that market represent?

Twenty-six to 30 million people;

Seventeen million eligible voters;

Thirty million dollars per month paid in union dues;

Millions of dollars contributed to pension funds;

Billions of dollars paid in local, state, and federal taxes;

A $145 billion English-speaking consumer market immediately accessible;

The most educated minds and the best trained labor force of any developing nation in the world;

A link and a bridge to the markets of other nonwhite developing economies (e.g., a half-billion Africans).[21]

He argues that America must move from the present racial battleground to economic common ground. It is difficult to do this, however, because most Americans do not see reality clearly.

The poor and the middle class have more in common than they have in conflict, and—though the short-term greed of the rich often prevents them from seeing it and keeps them resisting with all their might—such a coalition and change of course is in their long-term interest as well, because only productive, prosperous, and employed people can buy their products.[22]

Accordingly, Jackson calls for the creation of coalitions among the poor, the rejected, and the middle class. Feeding, clothing, housing, and educating the poor, he argues, would provide many needed jobs, and it would not distort the national economy the way favoring the rich and powerful does. Attention to the dispossessed and rejected ensures that they will take their place in political decision making. This leads both to a more stable political situation (because potentially dissident or revolutionary groups have been included and because injustice—the principal cause of unrest—is diminished) and to one which is more conducive to the progressive social change he seeks (because those most inclined to seek it have some political voice).

Finally, however, the movement from racial battleground to economic common ground is not sufficient. Americans also must move to higher moral ground.[23] This higher moral ground considers the common good rather than just private profit. National greatness, he argues, should be measured in moral as well as economic terms: "The new standard for measuring America's greatness must be how we treat children in the dawn of life; how we treat poor people in the pit of life; and how we treat old people in the sunset of life."[24] He believes that the common good, "the national interest, can best be served and protected with a coalition built from the bottom up."[25]

It follows from this, then, that for Jackson, moral and political arguments are interrelated. If a nation is to have political power at home and abroad, it first must have "moral authority," which he defines as believability and trustworthiness. He argues that it is essential for individuals and groups to rise above self-interest in order to achieve fulfillment. A nation can only ask people to do this if its leadership is viewed as having moral authority. And, as we will see in the discussion of foreign policy, the principal underutilized power which the United States possesses is moral authority.

EDUCATION

In addition to engaging in activities such as economic boycotts, he also preaches a message of hope and reform. These themes are especially prominent in his message to youth about educational reform. Reform in American education has been a major focus of his since 1975, when he began taking his message of equity, ethics, and excellence directly into high schools and also began addressing a wide variety of groups on this topic.[26] He typically addresses more than a hundred student groups each year.[27]

He argues that American public education is confronted by a dual crisis, one external, the other internal. The external crisis includes, first, racism, which "is still the number one impediment" to achieving a quality, effective public school system, and, second, an assault on the public economy, which includes an attack on the very notion that the community has a responsibility to provide quality public schools for all children. He argues that these two have come together in the last decade in what he calls "Bakkeism."[28] He uses this term to refer to the growing public resistance to the claims of blacks and other excluded groups that they should receive their fair share of the benefits of American society. He points out that the United States is in the process of creating a three-tiered educational system: a suburban school system based on class, a private school system based on race, and a public inner-city school system based on rejection and alienation. In short, because of racism and direct attacks on the public economy, blacks and other excluded groups are being denied the opportunity to secure a quality education.

But Jackson believes that "opportunity" is not enough. Education is confronted by an internal, as well as an external, crisis. "It is clear that not everything wrong with our schools is rooted in economic, social, legal, and political elements. . . . We need a revolution in values and priorities if we are going to turn the situation around."[29] He maintains that, as a first step, "effort must exceed opportunity for change to occur"[30] and argues that "moral decadence diverts one from the goal of catching up."[31] He therefore includes a number of elements in the internal crisis that he sees in public education: the loss of moral authority, moral decadence, mass-media diversion, a crisis in effort, and massive parental detachment. But in the final analysis, all of these come down to the loss of values and the loss of will. He exhorts people to "dig to new depths in order to penetrate the superficial" and "lift our sights in order to see a new vision."[32]

His message to youth includes a strong emphasis on hard work, self-discipline, and delayed gratification. He opposes explicitly suggestive language in popular music and the use of drugs and alcohol, and he preaches against a "teenage pregnancy epidemic." He typically employs slogans so his message can be easily remembered. To young people, he issues these challenges: "You can either use willpower on the inside and cope with or use pill power and cop out."[33] "You're not a man because you can make a baby. . . . You are a man because you can raise a baby and provide for a baby and develop a baby's life."[34] " 'Nobody will save us for us but us.' This means that nobody is going to register you for you. . . . Nobody is going to develop your mind for you but you."[35] "What does it matter if the doors of opportunity swing wide open and we're too drunk to stagger through them?"[36] "It's not my aptitude but my attitude that determines my altitude, with a little intestinal fortitude."[37] To both adult and youth audiences Jackson argues, we need "doctors who are more concerned with public health than personal wealth. Lawyers . . . who are more concerned with justice than a judgeship. . . . Teachers . . . who will teach for life and not merely for a living."[38]

Part of the crisis in public education arises, he maintains, from the misperceptions that education only takes place in the classroom and that schoolteachers are experts who have the sole responsibility for educating. He speaks to many of these misperceptions in his "Ten Commandments for Excellence in Education," which summarize much of his position:

1. Education is a task requiring total community involvement. It cannot be left solely to the public schools.
2. Parents are the foundation of education.
3. Public schools must define themselves clearly and say unequivocally what they stand for and believe.
4. High performance takes place in a framework of high expectation.
5. The laws of convenience lead to collapse, but the laws of sacrifice lead to greatness.
6. The death of ethics is the sabotage of excellence.
7. The full responsibility for learning cannot be transferred from students to educators.
8. Requiring students to do things that are demonstrably beneficial to them is not inherently undemocratic.

9. Learning will not take place if a disproportionate amount of school time and resources must be given to maintaining order.
10. All human beings, and especially young people, need to be involved in activities that provide a sense of identity and worth.[39]

To overcome the crisis in education, then, Americans must recognize the interrelationships that exist (1) between schools and communities, (2) among parents, educators, and students, and (3) between general societal values or expectations and educational achievement.

Thus he calls on the one hand for public policies that would provide for equal educational opportunity and on the other for a change in values and in will, both as a society and as individuals. This is why he calls for "equity, ethics, and excellence" in education. Opportunity is essential, but it is not enough. In education, as in other areas of life, Americans must address the issues of justice that lie beyond providing for equal opportunity.

Insofar as people listen only to his discussion of the internal crisis in American education, they can claim that his is a "conservative" approach, encouraging people to assume responsibility for their own lives and preaching the importance of high moral and ethical standards. As political columnist David Broder observed, "His 'Ten Commandments for Excellence in Education' could be endorsed by conservative Education Secretary William Bennett."[40] But, when viewed for its radical reconstitution of American values and policy, Jackson's program would bring about a new America, characterized by equity and parity.

POVERTY

Poverty is one of the issues he addresses most frequently. He often cites it as a prime example of the kinds of problems that people and governments ought to be concerned with or looks at its relationship to other problems, such as hunger or political unrest.

While some poverty may be due to lack of individual initiative, he focuses almost exclusively on such things as misfortune, unemployment, corporate policies, and government policies as the causes of poverty or as the means by which it is perpetuated. He typically emphasizes five key points when he addresses the issue of American poverty: (1) it is not necessary; (2) it is growing, not diminishing; (3) it is not spread evenly among various groups in America; (4) it is intimately related to many other American social problems; and (5) it can be eliminated.

Not only is poverty unnecessary in a country as wealthy as America, its presence is a judgment on this country's "perverted priorities." Although the numbers of the poor rose steadily in the first half of the 1980s, reaching a twenty-year high in 1985, "our government turned its back,"[41] taxing the poor more and eliminating or cutting back programs that aided them. For Jackson, this is a prime example of America's "civilizational crisis."

He notes that most Americans misperceive just who the poor are. Part of this is due to racism, and part to ignorance. Most poor people are not black, even though this is the perception. Thus he argues that America "must whiten the face of poverty. It's an American problem, not a black problem. But the face of poverty in this country is portrayed as a black face."[42] To make his point clear, he refers to a white entertainer who used to amuse white audiences by performing in blackface, pretending to be black but really being white. "We must remove the Al Jolson mask of poverty and show it for what it really is—a mainly white, female, and young phenomenon. . . . I must remind you that of those 35.3 million [poor], 24 million are white, 11 million are black, Hispanic, Asian, and Native American."[43] He notes that "seventy percent of all poor children live in a household headed by a woman" and argues that passage of the Equal Rights Amendment remains essential if that grim statistic is to be changed.[44] He also notes that, as with every negative fact of American life, blacks suffer disproportionately: blacks are twice as likely as whites to be poor; the income gap between black and white families has been increasing, black family income being just 55 percent that of white;[45] and black college graduates have about the same chance of being unemployed as white high-school dropouts.[46]

Poverty, he argues, is intimately related to such problems as hunger, high infant-mortality rates, poor education, and lack of political representation and power. It also is related to the tax code and government policies under Ronald Reagan which have reduced spending on social programs. Jackson notes, for example, that "the

1982 tax act shifted $20 billion from families already in poverty and gave an extra $64 billion to those who already made over $80,000 per year."[47] He also argues that poverty is closely linked to bloated military budgets. Contrary to the popular view, he argues that military spending is *not* good for the economy. Rather than creating jobs, "for every $1 billion spent by the Pentagon, 11,000 job opportunities are lost annually in the United States."[48]

In the final analysis, he concludes, poverty in this wealthy nation is a problem of priorities.

> We are not a poor nation forced to make choices between equally important goals, as some leaders would have us believe. . . . We don't have a resource problem. We have a priority problem—a moral problem. We have enough resources, but we waste them on bogus security. Our ultimate security is in our people and their well-being.[49]

He advanced a program for dealing with poverty in his 1984 campaign, one that illustrates well his 1988 "invest in America" campaign theme. This program called for cutting military spending by 20 percent, or $60 billion, without cutting America's defense capability. He would have done this by placing a freeze on nuclear weapons, cutting conventional weapons, ending waste and fraud, and renegotiating a reduction of U.S. military commitments in Europe and Japan.[50] He planned to use this $60 billion to begin the process of rebuilding America, putting Americans back to work doing socially useful and necessary work: building bridges and schools, employing teachers and nurses, ending the slums and ending poverty.[51]

HUNGER IN AMERICA

Throughout the 1980s, Jackson has championed the cause of family farmers hit by economic crisis during the presidency of Ronald Reagan. He appeared at rallies supporting farmers who were being forced out of business and gave numerous speeches on farm issues.[52] In these speeches, he argued that there is a link between "the rural feeders" and "the urban eaters,"[53] that farm issues are important to all Americans, not just to farmers.

In his view, nothing illustrates the crisis in American values better than the presence of hunger in this land of abundance. He argues,

Hunger and malnutrition in a wealthy nation don't just happen. They are caused. A study recently completed at the Harvard School of Public Health concluded that hunger has returned to America as a direct result of conscious government policies. As the economy weakened, as unemployment increased, as poverty rose dramatically . . . our government turned its back on our most needy, helpless, and vulnerable citizens.[54]

As he examines the problem of hunger, he sees it interrelated with several other problems—foreign trade policy, farm policy, the role of multinational corporations, monetary policy, hunger programs, poverty, urban unemployment, tax policy, racism, health care, and general foreign policy—and concludes:

We live in an interdependent society and an interdependent world. As the farm goes, so goes the city. We do not exist in separate oceans— one called "rural" and another called "urban"—and we are both in the same boat. When our small farms disappear, these proud, inde- pendent, but disillusioned and angry farmers will swarm to our cities to compete with black, brown, and poor unemployed workers for jobs that no longer exist—jobs that have been eliminated by automation or shifted to cheap labor markets abroad by the same corporate interests that took their farms. In the 1960s America responded to the hun- gry. . . . Serious hunger as a national problem was virtually elimi- nated. . . . [But] it is 1985, and hunger and malnutrition have returned as serious problems in America. . . . Hunger, of course, is related to poverty. And poverty today is significantly higher today than in any year since 1965. . . . I must remind you that . . . the poor are mainly white, mainly young, and mainly female. . . . Hunger has returned because the very programs which once virtually eliminated it were weakened and cut at the time they were needed the most. . . . It is a question of priorities. . . . Now is the time for leadership. Now is the time to choose. . . . Food and steel are the backbones of our national industries. . . . Together—farmers and steelworkers, rural and urban, black and white, male and female, young and old—we have a responsibility to save our farms and to ensure our steel industry's ability to grow. Both affect our national security. Both are sources of life. . . . The problems of Rainbow poverty, Rainbow unemployment, and the Rainbow loss of our family farms present us with the Rainbow challenge of 1985. Each of these elements of the Rainbow Coalition of the rejected crosses lines of race, sex, religion, and national origin. As people who love our children, who care about the future, who respect the earth and all of God's precious gifts, we must commit ourselves to ending hunger and malnutrition, to ending unemployment, and to saving the family farm and the farm family. Together we can save the farm and save the cities. Apart we can save neither.[55]

In this lengthy quotation, we can see not only Jackson's analysis of the problem of hunger but also an example of his general approach to all social issues. Whether the issue is black economic development, educational reform, poverty, or hunger, his analysis typically includes these seven elements:

1. The world is interrelated; both people and issues are interrelated in complex ways.

2. Change for the better ("progressive social change") is possible if people and governments will act. He is no believer in "fate" or in the benevolent workings of "the market" or the forces of history.

3. Because reality is interrelated, various "interest groups" actually have many interests in common. Thus coalitions among these groups are possible.

4. Beyond "interests," however, there is a "transcendent agenda" when seeking change—the full development of our individual and national powers. This agenda has its source in the values of the American dream, in Judeo-Christian values, and in the lessons of history.

5. Although a host of technical and political problems accompanies any social issue, at base every social issue finally is a question of priorities, it is a moral question. The technical and political problems can be solved once priorities are rearranged.

6. Americans often fail to perceive the interrelation of issues, the particular interests which groups have in common, and the possibilities for change that exist because Americans are blinded by cataracts of race, gender, or class.

7. Thus priorities and perceptions must be changed; America and Americans need to have their cataracts removed, to be converted to the transcendent agenda, to muster the determination to bring about change, and to begin the hard work of organizing people to bring about social change.

Other issues such as unemployment, environmental destruction, energy policy, or tax policy could be examined, but Jackson's analysis of each is much like the analyses of black economic development, educational reform, poverty, and hunger. Because each issue has a slightly different set of interconnections with other issues, there is a slightly different coalition of groups with a common interest in that particular issue. Otherwise, most of the analysis is similar to that given above.

The emphasis in Jackson's analysis is on principles, relationships, perceptions, and a vision of the common good rather than upon specific programs. The questions he continually asks are (1) which direction should we be going as a country?—emphasizing America the dream—and (2) in which direction are we now going?—emphasizing America the reality. The previous chapter on his vision of and call for a new America is not simply prologue to or background for understanding his political positions and proposals; it is an integral part of his approach to American politics. He believes that by focusing on principles, relationships, perceptions, and a vision of the common good Americans will be able to act more effectively in the political arena. This kind of focus allows citizens to view things in more holistic terms rather than in a piecemeal fashion. It helps citizens to understand the differences between various political programs and to evaluate these differences. His emphasis on perceptions involves helping citizens to see reality clearly, to understand their own self-interests, to see their common interests with others, and finally to see the value and wisdom of rising above their narrow self-interests to pursue the common good and create a new America.

As Barry Commoner observed: Jackson "makes people feel better about themselves because they can see how they are linked to others." But this feeling better is neither self-serving nor narcissistic: "Jackson's talent for challenging each group to look beyond the limits of its own, intense concerns is enormously important."[56] The coalitions he seeks to form are not simply for the purpose of advancing their own self-interests; they are to be "progressive coalitions," coalitions seeking fundamental changes in American life. Their focus is on creating a new America, characterized by the quest for "humane priorities at home and human rights abroad."[57]

4

Human Rights for All Human Beings: Reconceiving U.S. Foreign Policy

Some of Jackson's most controversial activities have been his trips abroad to meet with foreign leaders. In 1979 he traveled to several countries in the Middle East, and although he was denied the opportunity to meet with Israeli prime minister Menachem Begin, he did meet with Israeli opposition leader Shimon Peres, Jerusalem mayor Teddy Kolleck, and most notably with Yassir Arafat of the Palestine Liberation Organization. This meeting culminated in a widely circulated photograph of Jackson and Arafat hugging each other. In 1979 he also spent three weeks in South Africa. He met with Fidel Castro of Cuba in 1984 and negotiated the release of nearly fifty prisoners. In 1984 he also traveled to Nicaragua to meet with President Daniel Ortega. Each of these trips was highly publicized and highly controversial. His travels have also taken him to all the countries of the Middle East on more than one occasion, as well as to Panama, Mexico, the countries of Western Europe (including Scandinavia), Japan, South Korea, Morocco, Nigeria, the Congo, and all the countries of Southern Africa. He has met twice with Pope John Paul II at the Vatican and with the archbishop of Canterbury. In October of 1985 he had a widely publicized impromptu public meeting with Soviet General Secretary Mikhail Gorbachev, dealing with human rights, particularly those of Soviet Jews, at a time when Gorbachev was in Geneva to meet for the first time with U.S. President Ronald Reagan.

These trips abroad reveal much about Jesse Jackson's views on foreign policy, and no area of his work has occasioned more harsh criticism. The *New Republic,* for example, correctly notes that he challenges "what there is—or what there is left—of a national consensus on foreign policy," but it goes on incorrectly to claim that he espouses "views that are anti-democratic on the philosophical plane and anti-American on the strategic plane. . . . His is a Third World agenda."[1] His foreign policy views are fully democratic and thoroughly American, as will be seen in this chapter. No doubt much of this virulent criticism stems from the fact that—although there may not be a "national consensus on foreign policy"—there clearly is less pluralism in American politics about foreign policy issues than about domestic ones. Accordingly, challenges and deviations from this narrow range of acceptable positions are viewed as threatening. And there can be no doubt that he directly challenges the reigning "wisdom" about foreign policy issues and has chosen to make these particular trips abroad in large part to make public his challenge.

As he looks around the world, he sees all too many instances in which the United States has been "on the wrong side of history."[2] By this phrase, he not only means that, in international conflicts, the United States is backing the side that ultimately will lose—such as supporting Ferdinand Marcos in the Philippines—but more importantly he also means that the United States is backing the forces that in the long view of history will be seen as retrograde, regressive, and oppressive. He calls for a new course in American foreign policy, a foreign policy that is not foreign to American values.

> Public policy that sets the nation on a new course will put human rights over gunboat diplomacy and manifest destiny in foreign affairs. It will measure human rights and democracy by one yardstick. It will not define democracy as majority rule in America and as minority rule in South Africa. It will not side with the landed gentry over the poor and the disinherited. These regimes, born and bred in inequity, should not be supported by the United States. We who were born in revolution for freedom and equality surely must know and understand our own lesson in history, that, though the arc of the universe is long, it bends toward justice.[3]

How has the United States come to have such a misguided foreign policy? Although he believes there have been important differences between various administrations, he does not attribute a wrong-headed foreign policy to any particular president. As he puts it, "the . . . pilot may change with the various elections, but it is not merely the pilot that is in trouble—it is the ship."[4] American foreign policy, particularly since World War II, has been built on a "false vision."[5]

OBSTACLES TO CLEAR VISION

As he sees it, this false vision is a result of five things: (1) racism, (2) colonialism, (3) militarism, (4) a blind anti-communism, and (5) a foreign policy "realism" that lacks vision.

1. By far the most important among these, Jackson holds, is racism.

> The pathology of racism has been in the past and remains today the chief impediment in our striving for a more just and humane world in which to live. . . . Racism has blinded Europe, North America, and most of the "white Western world," and has left moral cataracts and scar tissue on our world eyes. Thus our vision . . . is blurred, unclear, and racist. . . . Racism as a cultural resource and sinful habit doesn't have much value as a medium of foreign exchange.[6]

The blurred vision caused by racism affects nearly every aspect of U.S. foreign policy and makes for glaring inconsistencies, such as defining democracy as majority rule in North America but as minority rule in South Africa.[7] Or, as he observes, "we should support a legitimate Solidarity labor movement and oppose martial law in Poland. But then we cannot become the number-one trading partner with South Africa when they impose martial law and violently crush a black solidarity labor movement."[8] Immigration policy likewise reflects America's positive regard for white peoples and negative regard for people of color. He argues, "we cannot have one standard for blacks and browns . . . and another for Europeans,"[9] yet this double standard is found throughout U.S. foreign policy.

2. Not only has the United States itself actually participated in colonialist activities during the past century much more than it believes it has, but U.S. foreign policy also has continued to support the Euro-American colonialist legacy. He points to country after country where, since World War II, the United States has supported the old colonial or colonial-based regimes rather than the indigenous

peoples in their struggles for freedom and self-determination.[10] Consequently, America too often has supported tyranny and autocracy rather than freedom and democracy.

Marvin Kalb's question at the opening of chapter 2—"Are your priorities, deep inside yourself, . . . that of a black man who happens to be an American or the reverse?"[11]—should be turned on its head and asked of U.S. foreign policy makers. Are American foreign policy makers white men who happen to be Americans or the reverse? Jackson concludes that there is far too much evidence that it is racism and identification with white Europeans, rather than American national interests, that dominate U.S. foreign policy considerations. No doubt this accounts for much of the intensity of the criticism of his approach to foreign policy.

3. Militarism rests on the assumptions that weapons are the ultimate power in resolving international disputes and that security can be obtained by military might alone. But as he continually points out, reality is constructed in just the opposite way: "ultimately, right is might; might is not necessarily right. And that which will be the ultimate power . . . will not be military authority, it will be moral authority."[12] "The guarantee of a nation's security is not ultimately the power of arms but the power of the spirit."[13] As he so often tells students, "there is nothing more powerful in the world than to be morally right."[14] Whenever military force is employed, it must be undergirded by moral authority. Jackson, who is not a pacifist, argues for using the least violent means possible in each situation, recognizing that even nonviolence involves a measure of coercion.

4. An unthinking, uncritical anti-communism keeps Americans from seeing the world as it is. It mistakes the causes of unrest and revolution and allows us to separate "ourselves from the decent opinions of humankind" and to make "a name for ourselves as international terrorists" by backing the anti-democratic forces simply because they bill themselves as "anti-communist."[15] Jackson notes that, "while there has been a tendency in both Republican and Democratic administrations of the past to see every foreign conflict . . . in East-West, U.S.-U.S.S.R. terms, under the Reagan administration this approach has been all consuming."[16] "When [Reagan] embraces dictators like Marcos, when he seeks to isolate Cuba and

make war on Nicaragua, he pushes the people of these nations into the arms of the Soviet Union."[17] Thus, he claims, the Reagan administration's obsession with communism is "self-defeating." Moreover, it results in self-contradictory behavior such as "declaring war on international terrorism and then mining the harbors of Nicaragua and financing attacks on its borders and the murder of its citizens."[18] He, however, recognizes that

> Communism is a real threat to peace and freedom in many places in the world today. But the United States cannot blindly embrace every anti-communist dictatorship in the world merely because it is anti-communist. Our foreign policy must have a consistent and real concern for human, worker, and political rights. Our national interest and security are best served by a consistent vigilance to the cause of human, worker, and political rights throughout the world, and when these rights are violated—whether by the right or by the left—our country ought to be found on the side of creative resistance to such violations.[19]

5. When he presents his vision of an interrelated, interdependent global community where countries relate to each other on the basis of mutual respect and reciprocity and where U.S. foreign policy is based on moral considerations as well as national interest, critics claim that he is being "unrealistic." Jackson responds by saying, "I want to remind you where excessive realism has taken us during the past forty years. . . . Realism without a vision is an empty process,"[20] for, as he reminds nearly every audience he addresses, "where there is no vision, the people perish."[21] This empty realism has kept American policy makers from seeing the tremendous power of ideals in the world and the strength of the will of oppressed people to be free.[22]

Thus the picture he paints is not that of an essentially sound foreign policy which has minor distortions because of racism, colonialism, militarism, blind anti-communism, and a visionless realism. Rather, it is one in which there is a great chasm between America the dream and America the reality. As things now stand, the United States sees itself as a "natural ally" of European nations, recognizing its links through immigration only with white nations. Latin America, Africa, and Asia are ignored. By being more anti-communist than pro-democracy and by using means that too often mimic those of our adversaries, much of U.S. foreign policy undercuts the very ideals of democracy. As a result, he notes that America too often has become "a helicopter gunship of despair" rather than "a beacon of hope" in the world and should return to being "a force for peace, for democracy, for human decency."[23] Distortions such as these do not lie at the periphery of American foreign policy, he concludes, they lie at its very center. Consequently, U.S. foreign policy needs to be reformulated so it can support, rather than hinder, American democratic values.

A variety of false perceptions results from these five obstacles to clear vision. Chief among these is the United States' inaccurate view of the rest of the world. The first step in developing a foreign policy, he proposes, should be "to count the foreigners." Of the five billion people in the world, half are Asians, "half of them Chinese. One of every eight people on earth is African."[24] Further, "most people in the world are neither white, Christian, English-speaking, nor rich. They are poor, black, brown, and yellow, and they yearn to be free."[25] Thus the first step toward clearer vision is to recognize the United States' minority position in the world numerically (as just 4 percent of the world's population), racially, religiously, linguistically, and economically.

Second, in spite of commonly used language that designates a "Free World," a "Communist World," or a "Third World," which suggests that there are several "worlds," Jackson maintains that America must recognize that we live in one world. And it is an interdependent world. "The world is interrelated, and its people are interdependent. Independence is an illusion, and isolation is suicidal."[26] Yet far too often the U.S. acts as if it does not need other countries and their good will, that it can operate independently. One reflection of this is the U.S. tendency to engage in bilateral rather than multilateral arrangements in foreign policy, such as offering direct financial aid to a country rather than working through international agencies such as the United Nations, the International Monetary Fund, or the World Bank. This illusion of independence is one source of American arrogance in foreign policy.

This illusion of independence and the tendency toward isolation lead to the third false perception: that there is a sharp line to be

65

drawn between U.S. foreign and domestic policy. He argues that "foreign policy grows out of domestic policy. We treat people abroad like we treat them at home."[27] Common wisdom has it that black Americans are concerned only with U.S. domestic policy. Yet as he points out, "we came here on a foreign policy."[28] He notes that those who make U.S. foreign policy fail to see the similarities between the struggles of black people in America and in South Africa.[29] He repeatedly points to the connections between U.S. tax policies for corporations which reward them for seeking cheap labor abroad and the problems in the automobile, steel, textile, rubber, electronics, and shoe industries at home.[30] He connects excessive military spending with failure to provide for America's poor and neglected.[31] He connects America's excessive deficit spending with the international monetary crisis threatening to bankrupt countries such as Brazil, Mexico, Argentina, Chile, and Peru.[32]

Militarism and blind anti-communism result in a fourth misperception by leading the U.S. to mistake the causes of unrest and revolution. "The roots of unrest," Jackson maintains, "lie in economic, social, and political problems. Hunger, disease, illiteracy, repression, and exploitation . . . [are] the reasons people rebel."[33] Security comes through justice[34] and through meeting people's basic human needs. "Educating our children, caring for the health needs of our citizens, providing safe and sanitary housing for everyone, and keeping our cities and industries strong are even more important in the long run to our national security than merely having a strong military defense."[35]

Finally, America's distorted vision results in a false perception of the proper roles of America in the world. Chief among these are America's roles as the world's police officer and as one of the world's chief arms suppliers. Too often America simply has played the role of bully, particularly in the Western hemisphere.

He summarized much of his position on foreign policy in an interview during the 1984 campaign:

> America looks upon the Third World with a lot of arrogance and contempt. Some of our contempt for Third World nations is based upon their poverty, some of it is based upon their color, some of it is built upon our relationship with the oppressors of those societies.

Some of it is based upon our corporations' exploitive relationship with those nations. The reasons we do this are essentially immoral or contemptuous. The Third World is mostly poor, uneducated, diseased, desperate for human rights, desperate for economic development, more inclined toward America than toward the Soviet Union. It's mostly black, brown, yellow, red, non-Christian, non-English-speaking.[36]

A NEW FRAMEWORK FOR U.S. FOREIGN POLICY

What is needed to remedy this deplorable situation, Jackson claims, is a new framework for foreign policy, which, in turn, demands a new vision of America and its role in the world. As with domestic problems, he claims that, at base, foreign policy problems are a result of misplaced priorities. Many of these grow out of the misperceptions that result from racism, colonialism, militarism, blind anti-communism, and a visionless realism. But one of the principal problems facing Americans in foreign policy questions is psychological. The U.S. must recognize the realities of the world as it exists in the 1980s, not pretend that this is still the 1940s or 1950s. The U.S. "must make the psychological adjustment from being superior over to being equivalent with and sometimes dependent upon" the rest of the world.[37]

As noted in the previous chapter, Jackson focuses not so much on specific programs as on principles and frameworks. By doing this he believes he can help Americans to see more clearly the basic principles and vision of America upon which various policies or programs rest, to see the relationships between apparently separate programs and policies, and to evaluate these policies and programs.

His new framework for U.S. foreign policy has four elements: (1) it rests on the affirmation of human rights for all human beings, (2) its goal is peace based on justice, (3) its means, as much as possible, are persuasive rather than coercive, and (4) it involves multilateral rather than bilateral approaches. Such a framework, Jackson maintains, would allow the U.S. to deal with the world as it presently is constituted, would realign U.S. foreign policy with American ideals, and would overcome the five obstacles to clear vision which distort American perception and U.S. foreign policy.

67

1. *Human Rights.* He believes that "human rights for all human beings" must be the central affirmation of any foreign policy. By being consistent and stressing human rights for *all* people, this approach opposes racism, colonialism, and America's blind anti-communism. The emphasis on human rights runs directly counter to approaches built on militarism and visionless realism. A foreign policy built on the concept of human rights affirms the importance and power of ideals and what he calls "moral authority." It recognizes the interdependent nature of the world and assumes the importance of self-respect and mutual respect.

2. *Peace with Justice.* This element in his framework directly opposes militarism as the principal basis for foreign policy because it insists upon justice as the basis for securing peace, but it also helps foreign policy makers break away from a blind anti-communism, and it also can oppose racism and colonialism. It recognizes the interdependence of apparently diverse issues and the interdependence of nations in the world, and it recognizes that the purpose of government is to serve all the people, not just the rich and powerful few. As Jackson argues:

> I see a great source of hope in the troubled relationship between our domestic policy and our foreign policy. . . . We need no longer believe that the interests of the people of this country are opposed to the interests of the people of other lands. We can open our hearts and our minds to the suffering of the people of Africa. . . . We can open our hearts to the "boat people" of Cambodia, the refugees from Haiti. [But] . . . unfair, unjust immigration policies represent no solution to the problems of plant closings. The workers who see their jobs exported to the Philippines, to Korea, to Honduras, to Haiti, and Guatemala cannot afford a foreign policy that props up right-wing dictators who torture trade union organizers in their own lands. The interests of the working in our own land will be far better served by a foreign policy that promotes the development of other nations than by desperate attempts to shore up our economy with "content legislation" and trade restrictions.[38]

3. *Persuasion Rather Than Coercion.* He argues that the means America employs must be consistent with the ends it seeks.[39] Using persuasive rather than coercive means implies a respect for the other party and involves attention to that party's needs and interests, and

it utilizes moral power along with military and economic power. In part, this accounts for his interest in meeting with foreign leaders, such as Yassir Arafat, Fidel Castro, and Daniel Ortega, usually shunned by U.S. political leaders.

4. *Multilateral Rather Than Bilateral Approaches.* Multilateral approaches recognize the interdependence of the peoples and nations of the world and the fact that not all international problems are to be understood fully in terms of the conflict between the Soviet Union and the United States. Thus he argues that any meaningful solutions to the problems of the Middle East, Central America, and Southern Africa will involve all the forces in those regions and their chosen leaders, especially the regional organizations such as the Contadora group, the Organization for African Unity, and the front-line states in Southern Africa. He also argues for strengthening and more fully utilizing the United Nations and for meeting with all the political leaders in an area where there is conflict, not just the ones the U.S. currently supports.[40]

CRITICAL FOREIGN POLICY AREAS

Jackson has concentrated his interest in foreign policy issues and has applied his framework for a new foreign policy in three areas where he believes the United States can make a difference: the Middle East, Southern Africa, and Central America. In each area, the obstacles to clear vision that he identifies make it difficult, if not impossible, for the United States to pursue its own national interests. In Israel, it is the American valuing of its white European immigrants, some of whom are Jewish, and not its people of color, some of whom are Arab. Thus American policy, as he sees it, has been more pro-Israel than it has been pro-peace. In Southern Africa, much the same situation obtains. There, U.S. foreign policy is aligned with the repressive white minority political leadership rather than with the black majority seeking human rights and freedom. In Central America, he believes, U.S. foreign policy is built on a blind anti-communism and on support for the landed gentry rather than for those seeking justice.

He made the first of his several trips to the Middle East in 1979.

69

He maintains that the United States has a vital interest in this area and that it should employ its diplomatic and economic strength to try to reconcile all the people of the region so that the cycle of pain can end.[41] He claims four elements are essential to any Middle East settlement:[42]

1. Israeli security within internationally recognized borders.
2. Self-determination or the right to a homeland.
3. Respect for the territorial integrity of Lebanon.
4. Normalization of relations between the U.S. and the Arab world.

The American goal in the Middle East should be peace because the continuing conflict is "costly, dangerous, and a detriment to the achievement of our vital interests in the region."[43] Jackson observes that half of all U.S. foreign aid goes to countries in the Middle East, that war in the Middle East threatens to widen into World War III, and that narrow but important national interests such as a stable oil supply are crippled by the inability to achieve peace. United States interests, such as they are, can only be made secure by the achievement of a lasting and just peace.[44]

Since his initial three-week visit to South Africa in July of 1979, he has talked about the "tragedy and treasure" of South Africa.[45] South Africa's treasure includes its mineral wealth, its strategic location at the southern tip of Africa, its industries, and its economy, but above all, its people, with their determination to be free. The tragedy, is, of course, the apartheid system. Apartheid is a system that does not recognize black humanity religiously, legally, politically, economically, or socially. Apartheid puts South Africa's economic and political arrangements in conflict with each other, but it also involves fundamental contradictions at every level of human life. In the long run, Jackson observes, "the human community cannot coexist with apartheid."[46] Compounding the tragedy of South Africa is the fact that the United States has been in partnership with South African apartheid. Not only has the United States been South Africa's number-one trading partner, thereby propping up its economic system, but by granting diplomatic recognition to the Pretoria government the United States helps legitimate the political system and, indeed, the entire apartheid arrangement.

He calls on the United States to be consistent in its foreign policy, to "measure human rights by one yardstick." Racism and a mindless anti-communism have blurred America's vision on human rights for black South Africans. Consistent with his general approach to social change, Jackson, upon his return from South Africa in 1979, noted that the United States had three options in dealing with South Africa: "luxury, leaving, or leverage."[47] Luxury would be to continue supporting and trading with South Africa; leaving would be to assume no moral, political, or economic responsibility for South Africa's future; while leverage, the option he advocated, would be for the United States to use all the power it has in the situation— diplomatic, economic, political, military—to bring about change that promotes justice and peace.

> Change is going to come in South Africa. Whether it will be essentially economic, political, and peaceful or whether violent and relatively sudden is yet to be determined. That lies largely in the hands of those with power in Pretoria. I am also convinced that the United States, for moral, economic, political, national interest, and national security reasons, ought to help facilitate the change there.[48]

In Central America, he advocates a similar position. Rather than defining the problems there as communists gaining a foothold in the U.S.A.'s backyard, he argues, "Central America is not our backyard, it is our neighbor. The cause of unrest there is not a Communist conspiracy, it is suffering and hardship, corrupt politicians, and repressive military dictatorships."[49] He supports the same goals and the same means to realize them in Latin America that he advocates for other areas of the world: peace based on justice; negotiations and mutual respect rather than gunboat diplomacy and military intervention; and support for human rights (measured by one yardstick) as the cornerstone of U.S. foreign policy. Thus in Central America and the Caribbean, he has called for normalizing relations with Cuba; engaging in and supporting negotiations to resolve the conflicts in Nicaragua and El Salvador; supporting the Contadora process; ending U.S. military assistance to the contras and to the governments of El Salvador and Guatemala; supporting Costa Rican citizens who oppose U.S. efforts to persuade the government of Costa Rica to raise an army; and assisting in development projects throughout the region.[50]

COMING TO TERMS WITH JACKSON'S FOREIGN POLICY

His approach to U.S. foreign policy alarms many because he so directly, forcefully, and persuasively challenges the "accepted wisdom" of the U.S. foreign policy establishment. In the arena of U.S. foreign policy, the five obstacles to clear vision that Jackson identifies—racism, colonialism, militarism, blind anti-communism, and an empty realism—constitute a direct attack both on accepted U.S. foreign policy and on those who make U.S. foreign policy. Neither "liberals" nor "conservatives" feel at ease being charged with these. Yet a thoughtful examination of the manifold and stark contradictions in U.S. foreign policy will show that these five obstacles are indeed plausible explanations for these contradictions.

His approach seems heretical when placed alongside current U.S. foreign policy, yet he seeks to offer a radical critique of current U.S. foreign policy by appealing to traditional American ideals and principles. Here again, he employs the dialectic between America the dream and America the reality. His emphasis in foreign policy on America the dream makes his opponents sputter. They charge him with being overly simplistic and naive, noting that reality is much more complex than his analysis would indicate and that traditional American ideals and principles simply do not apply in the foreign policy arena. He simply does not understand the complexity of reality, they argue. Indeed, by focusing on principles and on a framework for foreign policy rather than on the nitty-gritty details of particular policies themselves, his approach does appear simple. He argues, however, that it is this way so that it can be clear and so that the focus can be on the general direction of U.S. foreign policy. America will never get where it wants to go, he notes, until it starts going the right direction.

While his foreign policy framework is relatively simple, its implications are not. Negotiations based on mutual respect are more complicated than being the world's police officer or the Western hemisphere's bully. Human rights for all human beings is easy to articulate but much more difficult to implement.

His freewheeling, free-speaking, spontaneous personal style makes many people nervous and frightens others. His negotiating and debating skills clearly have had their successes, such as the release in January, 1984, of Navy Lt. Robert Goodman, who was being held captive in Syria after his plane was shot down, and Jackson's public dialogue with Soviet General Secretary Mikhail Gorbachev on human rights in Geneva in October 1985. Critics, however, wonder just when and in what ways he will breach the foreign policy consensus. It is worth noting that most of these critics had the same problems with Andrew Young when he was the U.S. Ambassador to the United Nations. In fact, however, most of the criticisms of Jackson's (and Young's) style actually are criticisms of the substance of what he has to say, of his insistence that America the reality be evaluated by America the dream.

Other criticisms or fears of Jackson emerge because he is black and chooses to address foreign policy issues. Recall, for example, the quotation from Marvin Kalb with which chapter 2 began: "Are your priorities, deep inside yourself, . . . that of a black man who happens to be an American or the reverse?"[51] This question is important because it expresses the fear that, deep down, black Americans may not have sufficient reason to be patriotic Americans, and because it articulates the widely shared belief that black people who are leaders are "black leaders," not simply "leaders." Coupled with this last matter is the belief that the only legitimate area of concern for "black leaders" is "civil rights," narrowly defined—the legal and political rights of citizenship. Thus black leaders, by definition, can have nothing legitimate to say about foreign policy. When Martin Luther King, Jr., chose to criticize U.S. involvement in the war in Vietnam, in part because of its racial dimensions,[52] he was severely criticized for going beyond the boundaries of his "legitimate" authority, namely, civil rights, narrowly conceived. Jackson addressed this general problem in the 1984 campaign by noting that reporters never referred to Gary Hart as a "white Colorado Senator" or to Walter Mondale as a "white former Vice President." Jackson argued that this is as it should be "because their whiteness is self-evident and my blackness is self-evident. When someone says 'black Jesse Jackson,' they're not trying to describe me; they are trying to define me and then confine me," to limit my universality.[53]

But Jackson, never one to be timid or falsely modest, also argues that his being black gives him a special point of view—indeed, a special advantage—in addressing questions of foreign policy. Black people "have been trained to be everything except diplomats, and yet it may be a skill born of a certain set of cultural experiences, and some survival needs for reconciliation, that makes us good and necessary diplomats. U.S. blacks are perceived on the world scene as conquering heroes, while whites are seen as pharaohs."[54] Here, he maintains, is another instance where the "rejected stones" are in a position to become the "cornerstone" for constructing a new America. But he correctly observes that white established political leaders have not welcomed this development:

> The fact of recognizing these rejected stones of previous generations, who are now the cornerstones of this generation, constitutes for many in the ruling class a state of cultural shock that has paralyzed the most developed minds of Western civilization. It has de-certified their private education and left them dizzy, staggering like a drunken man. They resist a world in which everybody is somebody. Being driven into an uncertain future against their will, they are being pushed forward but are reaching back, grasping for a relationship with the past that is nonnegotiable.[55]

The goal, Jackson argues, is for contributions of black Americans to foreign policy to be judged on their merits, not on the basis of who makes them[56] and to have a foreign policy that embodies the best, not the worst, of American values.

5

Progressive Social Change

Although Jesse Jackson has a religious-political vision of a just society and a peaceful world, it is evident that at present American society is not just and that the world is not peaceful. In order for these to be achieved, changes will have to occur. But, as he sees it, such changes involve more than modest adjustments in American society; they involve fundamental changes in many basic American institutions and values. That is why he calls himself a "progressive."

In spite of the call for fundamental changes in society, his vision is not utopian. He is a practical man with a realistic understanding of human nature and the limits of human possibilities. Rather than being wishful thinking, his vision provides standards for judging the present condition of American society and the world and also provides some guidance about how to change them.

He does not believe that justice and peace will be established through the outside intervention of God; nor will they be established through the natural progression of the laws of history or of some particular historical forces. Instead, he believes that a more just society and a more peaceful world can be established only through the strivings of human beings acting together on behalf of humane values. This is part of what is implied in his phrase, "nobody will save us for us but us."[1]

In order to understand what he means by progressive social change and how it can be brought about, it is useful first to examine his general view of reality.

JACKSON'S BASIC CONCEPTS

Self-Respect

Jesse Jackson's view of the nature of reality is founded upon his conviction that each individual is important and has integrity because each person is God's child.

> I believe that the lack of self-esteem—the feeling that "I" do not count, that "I" cannot make a difference—is one of the important losses of our day. I always begin my speeches to students with a chant entitled, "I Am Somebody." [This] litany is designed to say to all of us, I may be poor, uneducated, unskilled, prematurely pregnant, on drugs, or victimized by racism—whether black, brown, red, yellow, or white— but I still count. I am somebody. I must be respected, protected, and never neglected because I am important and valuable to myself and others. I am a unique and significant person with hopes, dreams, and aspirations that must be encouraged and developed, rather than crushed or ignored. The acceptance, in word and deed, of this idea and premise is the first step to achieving a brighter future. . . . People who feel good about themselves will care about and help other people.[2]

He argues that self-respect "is the most fundamental factor in one's mental and spiritual health"[3] and is the basis upon which mutual respect can be established. While he affirms the psychological value of self-respect, it is the theological or spiritual value that finally matters. Racism is theologically wrong because it denies the idea that all people are valuable because they are God's children. As he sees it, a black person's act of resisting racism is an affirmation of self-worth that is both religious and psychological. Resisting racism also is a highly political act in whatever context it occurs because it denies the legitimacy of all social arrangements based on racism.

His understanding of human nature is usually called "realistic." That is, he believes that human beings are neither essentially "good" nor essentially "bad" or "evil." Rather, they are a complex mixture of the two. "There is some of the best in the worst of us and some of the worst in the best of us."[4] "All of us have strengths and weaknesses. None of us is whole," he says. "All of us are crippled or handicapped in some way."[5] He recognizes the immense power of self-interest, but he also believes "sacrifice" and a "higher ground" beyond self-interest are essential parts of human nature. While recognizing and then advancing one's own self-interest is the starting point for all social action, achieving self-interest cannot be the entire purpose of action. There is a "higher ground" that must be sought if fulfillment is to be achieved. He illustrates the interplay of these various aspects of human nature when he discusses the idea of "service:"

> Some may say, "Now, Reverend, that service and altruism stuff is idealistic and naive. Don't you know mankind is basically selfish?" The principle of service takes humanity's selfishness and need for self-fulfillment into account. If need is the basis of social organization, and serving that need is power, it is also true that self-interest is the sustaining force. Even Jesus recognized this trinity when he said, "Love your neighbor as yourself." Love is the most basic human need. To serve your neighbor (in the spirit of love) is to love your neighbor. And it is impossible to help others without helping yourself in the process—just as it is impossible to hurt others without hurting yourself. So service is the means of loving your neighbor as you love yourself. . . . The principle of service, then, doesn't deny the needs of self and ego and does not deny the need for power; rather it affirms their fulfillment in the highest and best manner.[6]

As will be discussed below, self-interests need to be met, but they also need to be relativized and transformed by what he calls "vision" if human fulfillment is to be realized.

The Interrelation of All Reality

As was discussed in more detail in chapter 2, Jackson believes all of reality is interrelated. Individual differences and needs are important and need to be recognized, but finally all people and all institutions and all dimensions of life are interrelated. As he noted in his speech at the 1984 Democratic National Convention, "America is not like a blanket, one piece of unbroken cloth—the same color, the same texture, the same size. It is more like a quilt—many patches, many pieces, many colors, many sizes, all woven and held together by a common thread."[7] The image he most frequently uses to express this interrelatedness is, of course, the rainbow. Quilts and rainbows are things in which both the individual parts and the larger patterns can be seen and are important.

But it is not just individual people or groups of people who are interrelated. All of reality has this character. For example, in a 1984 campaign speech in Akron, Ohio, he outlined the connections he saw between several apparently separate issues. He connected the loss of twenty-five thousand jobs in the rubber industry in Akron with U.S. tax policy; multinational corporations' search for higher profits by exporting jobs abroad to cheap labor markets; U.S. foreign policy; the federal government's budget deficits; the abdication of governmental responsibilities for domestic needs such as education, cleaning up the environment, and rebuilding cities and roads; resistance to affirmative action programs; and the current hostility toward labor unions.[8]

However, because Americans have forgotten their relationship to each other and the interrelated nature of the world, they often are unable to deal effectively with many social problems. In order to bring about change, he argues, these interrelationships must be rediscovered: "Even in our fractured state, all of us count and fit in somewhere. We have proven that we can survive without each other. But we have not proven that we can *win* or *make progress* without each other."[9] Because each person has strengths and weaknesses, "All of us need to use our strengths to heal and mend the weaknesses and infirmities of others and to be healed by the strengths of others."[10] When looking at social problems, he notes:

> The tasks before us—a new foreign policy, a new domestic policy, decent schools, a clean environment, a safe and inexpensive energy program—look impossible if we face them one at a time, if we face them alone. . . . Each problem that we face as a nation is related to every other problem. It is our task to define that relationship.[11]

These various interrelationships provide the possibility for forming coalitions.

Vision

In Jackson's understanding of reality, "vision" is a crucial concept because it is necessary for human fulfillment. Vision also introduces much of what makes him distinctive among American political leaders. He frequently quotes Prov. 29:18 (KJV): "Where there is no vision, the people perish." Vision serves two main purposes for him: it provides insight by allowing people to see beyond the present situation, and it provides the basis for individual and societal fulfillment.

Sometimes he talks about vision as "the dream that sustains us through the dark times and the dark realities. It is our hope."[12] "Don't let them break your spirit,"[13] he advises those seeking social change. The conclusion of his speeches typically contains this line: "I believe that suffering breeds character, character breeds faith, and in the end faith will not disappoint."[14] Thus vision provides hope and the grounds for perseverance.

In a related vein, he says in his political campaigning, "Our party must not only have the courage and the conscience to expose the slummy side. We must have the conviction and vision to show America the sunny side, the way out."[15] As he puts it directly: "I'm not talking about eyesight; I'm talking about insight."[16] Vision, he asserts, "can lift you above misery to miracles and allow you to smile through tears."[17] Vision thus points beyond the current problems and realities of life to the enduring nature of reality itself, a reality which, for him, includes a God of justice who is in control of the universe.

Vision does this in part by helping people see reality without distortion. In his 1984 campaign, for example, Jackson believed that Americans' sight was being distorted by racism, nationalism, and false religious appeals and argued:

> We must remove the cataracts of race from the eyes of our people and lift them out of poverty, ignorance, disease, and fear. . . . We must not blind them with prayer clauses, drape them in flags, and give them hot feelings of false racial pride when they remain hungry, ignorant, and diseased in the wealthiest nation in the history of the world.[18]

Vision also provides the basis for human fulfillment, for going beyond narrow self-interest. Although self-interest is the first principle of political activity, he argues that politics finally must be informed by something more than self-interest—by vision. Perhaps the phrase that best expresses this idea is his call for Americans to "move from racial battlegrounds to economic and political common ground and moral higher ground."[19] Without this call, he could be viewed as a typical interest-group politician (although a black one), advancing the interests of the particular group he represents. With it, however, he becomes a person calling for a transformation of American politics as it currently exists—a politician calling for Americans to "go another way." He also becomes an enigmatic and controversial political figure because most political analysts believe that the only reality in politics is self-interest. Nothing else, they argue, really has any effect, and any other appeals to citizens, such as appealing to notions of a "common good," are simply ways to disguise or legitimate advancing one's own or one's group's own self-interests. But he contends: "realism without a vision is an empty process."[20]

Vision provides the standards for evaluating individual and even national fulfillment. To individuals, he offers this challenge:

> Live beyond the pain of reality with the dream of a bright tomorrow. Use hope and imagination as weapons of survival and progress. . . . Young people, dream of a new value system. Dream of teachers, but teachers who will teach for life, not just for a living. . . . Dream of a world where we measure character by how much we share and care, not by how much we take and consume.[21]

Jackson argues that America's "greatness must be measured by our ideals . . . and how closely we approximate them."[22] He describes his vision of a transformed American society, of America the dream, most forcefully when he calls for redefining "national greatness":

> It's not the size of our GNP. It's not our military might. It's not our educational and technological achievements—as great and as necessary as each of these may be. More fundamental to greatness, by my definition, is how we treat children in the dawn of life, how we treat poor people in the pit of life, and how we treat old people in the sunset of life. If we treat them with respect and dignity, we'll be a great nation. If we care for our young, insuring their proper nutrition and educate them to work in tomorrow's world, we'll be a great nation. If we provide decent, safe, and sanitary housing and food for the poor, then we'll be a great nation. If we provide health care and food and show respect for our elderly and allow those who are able and willing to continue to contribute something meaningful to our society, then we'll be a great nation. Greatness is in how we value and care for our people.[23]

Beyond the notions of freedom and self-determination that grow out of his conviction that each person is somebody worthwhile whose needs deserve to be taken seriously, he also emphasizes the concepts of "sacrifice" and "unearned suffering," both of which are related to vision. Sacrifice has two meanings for him. First, he uses the term to mean giving up something in the short term in order to gain something of worth in the long term: "Anything worth having is worth working for above and beyond the call of duty."[24] As expressed in the fifth of his "ten commandments" for excellence in education: "The laws of convenience lead to collapse, but the laws of sacrifice lead to greatness." He continues, "Anything that is conveniently achieved has low market value. . . . You become successful in music, art, science, politics, athletics, marriage, and in life itself because you sacrifice."[25] Although sacrifice here seems to have more to do with delayed gratification than with specifically religious ideas, he is pointing to the importance of seeking the broader humane values and ideals which vision allows a person to see, as opposed to seeking self-fulfillment understood as hedonistic self-gratification.[26] This is the second and more fundamental meaning of sacrifice for him: seeking the common good and humane values rather than narrow self-interest. Thus sacrifice is the way that self-interest becomes transformed when people have vision. He argues that human fulfillment lies on a "higher ground" beyond self-interest.

Suffering—particularly unearned suffering—has a clear religious meaning for him. Two statements about suffering reappear throughout his speeches: "Unearned suffering is redemptive"[27] and "Suffering breeds character, character breeds faith, and in the end faith will not disappoint."[28] Both of these rest upon Jackson's belief that, in the end, God is in control of the universe and that this God is a God of justice.

> In your dreaming you must know that unearned suffering is redemptive. Water cannot wash away the blood of martyrs. Blood is thicker than water. Water makes grass and flowers grow, but blood makes sons and daughters of liberation grow. No matter how difficult the days and dark the nights, there is a brighter side somewhere. In Angola, Mozambique, Nicaragua, El Salvador, South Africa, Greenville, South Carolina, and Harlem, there is a brighter side.[29]

Without question, his view of reality is highly religious, although it often is not articulated in specifically religious terms. It rests upon a belief in a God of justice who finally is in charge.[30] This God can

81

be seen only if people have vision. This same God also is the source of worth for individuals (all people have value because they are children of God) and is the basis for the interrelationship between individuals and groups (all people are brothers and sisters because all are God's children).

PROGRESSIVE SOCIAL CHANGE

Once his most basic beliefs are examined, it is easier to understand his view of society and social change. Because each individual is important, social change can come from the "bottom" of society as well as from the "top." Because both people and issues are interrelated, coalitions are possible. And because of vision, people are able to rise above self-interests to what he calls "moral higher ground." His view of progressive social change will be examined in four parts: the dialectic between opportunity and effort, the place of self-interest, the means available for creating social change, and the ends sought.

The Dialectic between Opportunity and Effort

As Jackson sees it, all change involves a dialectic between "effort" and "opportunity." This is a dialectic between motivation and circumstances. His basic formula is: "effort must exceed opportunity for change to occur."[31] He agrees with conservatives in believing that hearts and minds must be changed if there is to be social change, but he also agrees with liberals in insisting that changes in institutions and public policies are essential. He believes that changed minds and changed institutions are both necessary: "We must wrestle with unjust structures, not merely with unjust men."[32] This is part of the reason he avoids current political labels and calls himself a "progressive."

In his approach, however, changing hearts and minds includes more than just changing individuals. Groups and even nations can change their hearts and "go another way." "Conversion means a change of heart. That's what America needs—conversion from a despairing society to a caring society."[33] "Our struggle," he says, "is . . . to change the character of our nation."[34] When he examines national purpose, he is raising questions about national will and national priorities—all a part of "effort," as he sees it. We must, he says, "try to get the nation to again focus on the big picture. What are our priorities? What is the budget trying to achieve? How does it measure up to the historic ideals of the country and its people?"[35] Thus *all* change—individual change and change in societies—involves this dialectic between motivation and circumstances, between effort and opportunity.

Jackson illustrates this dialectic when he addresses educational issues. The first problem to be addressed, he argues, is the public policy question of equal educational opportunity, of equal access to quality desegregated multicultural education. But, while this is essential, it alone is not enough. "What does it really matter if we have a new book or an old book if we open neither? Motivation is at least as important as opportunity."[36] He declares that "excellence is doing your best—as an individual or a nation—against the odds"[37] and speaks of "sin" as "doing less than your best."[38] He argues that there is a "correlation between pressure and progress."[39] Thus he simultaneously argues for changing public policies and changing hearts and minds, rather than simply addressing one or the other. Change is not complete unless both occur.

While both kinds of changes may be equally important in some abstract sense, changed hearts and minds do seem to be more important to him than changed institutions in at least two respects. First, as he views it, changed hearts and minds typically are chronologically prior to changed institutions. They come first. They are required in order to create the pressure necessary for initiating social change. "We need a sober, sane, and disciplined army to catch up,"[40] he argues. "A handful of sober and sane people wield more power than densely populated cities of drugged and alienated people."[41]

Second, and more important, he believes that freedom has an internal, not an external, source. "Freedom originates in the mind and the will. We can never be made truly free from without," he says. "If our minds are not free, then they can remove the chains of slavery, but we will still be in bondage. However, if our minds are free and our spirits determined, no external force can enslave us."[42] Thus he argues, "It's bad to be in the slums, but it's even worse when the slums get in you. If you get your willpower, you can be in the slums without the slums being in you. You can transform that slum."[43] In short, "no power is more fundamental than willpower."[44] Freedom comes from within and comes in spite of circumstances. Circumstances alone never can make people free, either individually or corporately.

This internal freedom, this self-determination, also is the basis for rising above adversity, for making progress even when running "against a headwind." "With a made-up mind, which is the most powerful instrument in the world, you can rise above your circumstances."[45] Thus he tells students that "it is not [their] aptitude but [their] attitude that will determine [their] altitude, with a little intestinal fortitude."[46] This is not so much a statement of optimism as it is a recognition that "achievement in critical areas is always against the odds, always against headwinds."[47] Not only is this true of all individual achievements, but he also emphasizes that "the freedom struggle is always against the headwinds."[48] "Those of us who are behind must get up earlier, we must work harder, we must be more determined, more humane, more sober, more sane, and more sensitive."[49] This has been his message to America's disinherited for more than two decades. This is the challenge for them that lies beyond opportunity. It is the challenge of effort and discipline to take advantage of existing opportunities and to press for more en route to the goal of equity and parity in all areas of American life.

Because changed hearts and minds play such an important role in Jackson's view of progressive social change, he has been criticized by people who mistakenly believe he has "blamed the victim" rather than the victimizer for social injustices. To these critics, he responds:

> I'm not arguing that the victimizers abdicate their responsibility, and I challenge victimizers everywhere I go. While I know that the victimizers may be responsible for the victims being down, the victims must be responsible . . . for initiating change, determining strategy, tactics, and timing, and being disciplined enough to pull it off. No one has a greater self-interest than the victims in getting up, while the victimizers do not perceive it to be in their self-interest.[50]

Thus the starting point in his analysis of what is required for progressive social change is this dialectic between opportunity and effort, between circumstances and motivation. Opportunity must be present, but it alone is not enough. Effort must exceed opportunity if change is to occur, and both must be present for change to be complete.

The Place of Self-Interest

Jackson contends that self-interest is the basis for all political organizing[51] and that change comes from the bottom up. "No . . . godfather is going to wake us up one night and save us from this nightmare. No Savior will ascend to the throne in the White House. Nobody will save us for us but us."[52] Using other imagery, he concludes:

> To expect change to come . . . from the top down is a false expectation. . . . It is unrealistic to think that the slave master will voluntarily bring an end to slavery. Freedom does not come from the Big House or the White House but from your house and my house. . . . There is a greater correlation between pressure and progress than there is between presidents and progress.[53]

Change comes from the bottom up not because those on the bottom are more enlightened or more meritorious than others but because change clearly is in their self-interest.

> The slave master may adjust if the slave changes his mind and revolts, but the slave master will never voluntarily initiate an end to slavery. He does not perceive it as being in his self-interest to do so. Slave rebellions, not slave masters, freed the slaves.[54]

Looking at self-interest in a somewhat narrow way, he argues: "It is not to anyone else's self-interest for us to make adequate wages but us. It is not to anybody else's self-interest for us to take over their company but us. It is not to anybody else's self-interest for us to become mayor but us."[55]

Jackson, however, as noted earlier in the section on "vision," typically employs a much larger view of self-interest, distinguishing between short-term and long-term self-interests and between clearly understood self-interests and interests that are hidden from the self because the "cataracts" of race, class, or sex have distorted a person's vision. People often have to have these "cataracts" removed before they can first recognize and then act on their self-interests. (Note that this again calls for the primacy of changed hearts and minds.)

His political speeches typically combine these various elements into a single argument:

> There are too many unregistered and non-participating potential poor voters, and there are too many poor and middle-class voters voting for the interests of the rich. The rich use the middle class as a buffer against the poor, but the national interest can best be served and protected with a coalition built from the bottom up. The poor and the middle class have more in common than they have in conflict, and though the short-term greed of the rich often prevents them from seeing it and keeps them resisting with all of their might—such a coalition and change of course is in their long-term interest as well, as only productive, prosperous, and employed people can buy their products.[56]

Because the vision of so many Americans is obscured by race, sex, or class, he argues that much needs to be done to help them understand just what their own true economic and political interests are. Because they actually hold many economic and political interests in common, America's rejected peoples need to form coalitions to advance these common interests. Thus he calls for a rainbow coalition of the rejected, not a melting pot, because these needs and interests must be met, not melted.

The Means for Social Change

One of his basic ideas is that reality—rather than being composed of separate spheres of life—is interrelated. As a result, creating change in one area of life (improving education, for example) makes possible changes in other areas (such as opening up various occupations and professions to previously excluded people). These changes then may create other changes (such as higher economic status and the ability to purchase better housing).

This fairly common way of viewing reality and social change was given one of its most full theoretical descriptions by Gunnar Myrdal in his massive study, *An American Dilemma*. He calls this way of looking at change the "principle of cumulation" and notes that it can work in either a positive or a negative direction. The negative direction often is popularly referred to as a "vicious circle." A change in any one factor or area of life, "independent of the way in which it is brought about, will . . . start the whole system moving in one direction or the other."⁵⁷ This summarizes well Jackson's approach to creating progressive social change: changes in one area of life make possible changes in other areas.

One consequence of this approach is that Jackson does not look for one single, basic, predominant, or key factor that causes racism or that must be dealt with if any progressive change is going to occur.⁵⁸ Rather, the key to bringing about change is to use *whatever* levers for change are available—economic, political, legal, or educational—and to confront racism in *whatever* area of American life it appears. Such an approach, of course, means that his position on issues can appear fluid, even inconsistent, and that he can appear to be a highly political rather than a clearly principled actor, a charge that will be examined in detail in the next chapter.

He is a pragmatist. As he has said of himself:

> I am not a political purist; I'm a political activist. I make political decisions. I choose to vote in an imperfect political system because I'm a political activist. I deal with Democrats, Republicans, non-aligned, unregistered, and disinterested because I am an activist. I am involved in the affairs of my day. I am not a referee, not an arm-chair philosopher, not a grandstand spectator. I believe in activity.⁵⁹

He is not wedded to any particular method or ideology in attempting to achieve his ends, as long as the means he employs are consistent with the ends he seeks. This pragmatism frustrates both friend and foe whenever they wish him to have a consistent ideology or program for change. For example, he is not a socialist, and he is not a capitalist. But he is willing to use elements from either approach insofar as they assist him in his goals of opposing racism and creating a more just society and a more peaceful world.

His attempt to form a Rainbow Coalition of the rejected is his attempt to bring together all those who recognize that they have a self-interest in bringing about progressive social change. He listed the potential members of such a coalition in his speech before the Democratic National Convention in 1984:

> The white, the Hispanic, the black, the Arab, the Jew, the woman, the Native American, the small farmer, the businessperson, the environmentalist, the peace activist, the young, the old, the lesbian, the gay, and the disabled make up the American quilt.⁶⁰

Jackson argues that America's rejected hold the keys to progressive social change. Using biblical imagery, he claims that these "rejected stones can become the cornerstones of a new progressive coalition in America who will help to reshape a new domestic and world order."[61] Many, however, wonder how these rejected groups could possibly bring about such massive changes. He replies with more biblical imagery: "We must focus on the strength and courage of David, not just on the tyranny of Goliath. . . . David has unused rocks just lying around. Goliath [intimidated] with a perverse coalition of the rich and the unregistered."[62] Among the most important of these "unused rocks" that Jackson points to is the ballot. He notes that in 1984, for example, eighty-five million people—47 percent of the eligible electorate—did not vote in the presidential election, and fifty-four million of these people were not even registered. Thus even the Reagan "landslide" did not involve a majority of the eligible electorate. The ballot is such a powerful tool for change, Jackson argues, because the old minorities actually constitute a new majority. Other powers the disinherited possess include consumer power, litigation, various forms of moral persuasion, direct action, and—above all—the power of moral authority, by which he means the ability to be believed, trusted, and respected. Moral authority, in his view, is the ultimate power, the power that can defeat armies and governments.[63]

Each of these powers that rejected peoples may possess is dramatically increased whenever coalitions are formed. Thus, as a first step to meeting their own needs, America's rejected must form a rainbow coalition of the rejected. Such a coalition would be based on self-interest, because, as he understands it, self-interest is the basis for all political organizing. But such a rainbow coalition also must be based on self-respect because without self-respect people do not recognize the validity of their own interests or the extent of their own powers.

He then calls for creating a second kind of coalition. The rainbow coalition of the rejected needs to join with others seeking progressive social change and finally with the middle class. This coalition also would be based in part on self-interest. To these people who are not among America's rejected, he argues that race, class, and sex have distorted their vision and have kept them from seeing their true self-interests. But, in seeking to build this second kind of coalition, he also appeals to the interrelated nature of reality. Recall part of his argument, quoted earlier:

> The poor and the middle class have more in common than they have in conflict, and—though the short-term greed of the rich often prevents them from seeing it and keeps them resisting with all their might—such a coalition and change of course is in their long-term interest as well, because only productive, prosperous, and employed people can buy their products.[64]

Entering into coalitions, however, is not without pitfalls. He often sounds a cautionary note: be clear about your own interests, and don't let your sight be obscured or diverted by others. For example, he argues:

> As black people, we have only varying degrees of access to the Republican and Democratic vehicles. But we can't ride to freedom in Pharaoh's chariot. Neither vehicle has as its primary commitment our liberation and development. . . . It is better that we lose a political race and keep our self-respect than to win the race and lose our soul.[65]

During Jackson's public career, he has employed and argued for each of the various powers listed above (political, consumer, legal, etc.) as ways of bringing about progressive social change. Except for moral authority, which always must be present, no single one of these powers holds the key to change. He argues for using whatever power is at hand. As he said to the Republican National Committee in 1978:

> Power is simply the ability to achieve purpose. Our purpose [as black people] is both simple and complex. Simple because our goal is equity and parity (our share). Complex because we must begin where we are and use what we've got to take us to where we want and need to go.[66]

But power alone is not enough. Leverage is also required. People have maximum leverage when they have enough power to determine where the balance of power will lie. As he told the Americans for Democratic Action:

> Black people must pursue a strategy that prohibits one party or one element within a party from taking us for granted or another party or element from writing us off. . . . If we follow a strategy of blindly giving our vote to one political faction, we will have power but no

leverage. If we write any particular element off, we again sacrifice leverage. So "power" or "no power" will not allow us to pursue our vested interests if we do not have *leverage*.[67]

This same strategy applies to the economic realm as well as to the political. Black consumers often account for sales far in excess of the margin of profit. Thus, because they possess leverage, a small, disciplined group can bring about a great deal of change.

Note that violent means are not included in the list of powers which Jackson believes black and rejected people potentially possess. In part this is because the same nation which has rejected these people possesses a monopoly of the weapons of violence; thus rejected people do not have access to the weapons of violence. But much more than this, he rejects violence because he believes that corrupt means also corrupt the people who use them. As he says, "you cannot hold someone in the ditch without lingering there with them."[68] "It is impossible to help others without helping yourself in the process—just as it is impossible to hurt others without hurting yourself."[69] He holds that the means by which people live "must be consistent with the ends for which they live."[70] These statements are all ways he has of referring to what he calls the "divine law of reciprocity,"[71] a law which rests on the confidence that, in the long run, a God of justice will prevail.

Yet he is no pacifist, trusting only in God to set things right in the long run. He argues for using the least violent means possible in any situation, but he recognizes that this will vary with the circumstances. Nonviolent means are preferable to violent ones because they do less injury, but circumstances do not always allow them.

In sum, his approach to social change involves three steps. First, rejected people must change their minds about themselves and recognize that they are important rather than impotent. Second, through self-discipline, they must develop and organize whatever powers and resources they possess. Third, they must use this power to gain leverage to bring about changes.

Ends

The kind of change he seeks is a "renegotiation" of the current arrangements in society which favor certain people based on their race, sex, or class. The goal is equity and parity in all areas of life, a just society and a peaceful world. In overcoming America's racism, Jackson argues for a "quilt," not a "blanket" or a "melting pot." He calls for an integration which is not equivalent to assimilation. But making this argument is as difficult in the 1980s as it was in the late 1960s, when the options seemed to be either assimilation or separation.

As usual, Jackson has employed several images to assist him in making his case. In the 1980s he has been using the images of a quilt and a rainbow to symbolize the complex, integrated interrelation that the many American peoples have. Rather than homogenizing everyone—subordinating their distinctive histories, strengths, problems, and contributions to the "common good" and destroying their uniqueness in the process—he instead calls for a recognition of individual and group differences. But then he also calls for relativizing them in light of the larger goal of the "common good." The United States, he declares, "should continue to make even greater strides and progress toward achieving the ideal 'rainbow' nation, . . . weaving a beautiful national quilt of races, varied cultural origins, religious persuasions, colors, political parties, geographical distribution, income levels, professions, and occupations."[72] When it comes to the international level, he describes a world at peace as

> a world which recognizes itself as interdependent, yet accepts and affirms the uniqueness and self-dignity of each nation and culture. It will be a world in which justice rather than power orders the relationship between nations great and small and in which the problems of a millionaire businessman, an unemployed steelworker, and a starving child in Africa are all treated with equal concern.[73]

In political language, he argues that politics does not involve the question of whether to advocate one's own self-interests *or* the common good; rather, politics involves both self-interests *and* the common good in a complex relation. Along with most political analysts, he recognizes that much of the political rhetoric about the "common good" in American political life is simply an attempt to disguise the self-interests of the rich and powerful and to render invisible and illegitimate the self-interests of the poor and powerless. Accordingly, he argues that self-interests and recognition of differences must be brought to the surface and should not be totally subsumed under notions of the common good. To subsume them would be to deny their legitimacy, however limited, and to bring about their elimination by assimilating or homogenizing them in a "melting pot" whose principal ingredients have been decided by others.

Most contemporary political theorists and analysts transfer the economic model of the free market to the political realm. They argue that politics is a neutral mechanism for settling differences that exist among various self-interests. Politics is thought to automatically promote the common good, understood as the sum of individual self-interests. Jackson, however, believes in a common good which is distinct from the sum of individual or group self-interests and which must be directly pursued. It does not automatically result from seeking self-interests. Thus he calls for an activist, caring government rather than a laissez-faire one.[74]

Similarly, he argues that justice, including racial justice, lies beyond self-interest and is not a substitute for it. The legitimate claims of self-interest must be dealt with before a person can rise above or go beyond them. Thus his goal in terms of racial justice is not so much a "color-blind" society as it is a society where all racial groups are valued and where racial justice is present—a quilt, not a melting pot.

Some of the confusion about how to regard him grows out of a clear tension in his own approach to achieving racial justice. He employs much of the rhetoric of "black power" advocates who call for developing the distinctive resources of American black people, often relatively independent of the rest of American society, when he declares "I am somebody," when he calls for black economic development based on self-reliance, when he announces that "our time has come," or when he concludes "nobody can save us for us but us." In addition to this kind of language, however, he also argues for black Americans' full participation in all aspects of American society, calling for "equity," "parity," and "reciprocity."

He is not to be faulted for this tension in his language and approach. There always has been a dialectic in the black community in America between these two approaches.[75] The dialectic, however, does not indicate an inconsistency in black Americans' approach to achieving racial justice; rather, it grows out of the reality of the black experience in America. It was given its classic description by W. E. B. DuBois in 1903 in his essay on the "double consciousness" of American black people:

> One ever feels his two-ness—an American, a Negro; two souls, two thoughts, two unreconciled strivings; two warring ideals in one dark body, whose dogged strength alone keeps it from being torn asunder.
>
> The history of the American Negro is the history of this strife—this longing to attain self-conscious manhood, to merge his double self into a better and truer self. In this merging, he wishes neither of the older selves to be lost. He would not Africanize America, for America has too much to teach the world and Africa. He would not bleach his Negro soul in a flood of white Americanism, for he knows that Negro blood has a message for the world. He simply wishes to make it possible for a man to be both a Negro and an American, without having the doors of Opportunity closed roughly in his face.
>
> This, then, is the end of his striving: to be a co-worker in the kingdom of culture, to escape both death and isolation, to husband and use his best powers and his latent genius.[76]

In this passage, DuBois rejects both the "isolation" of separation and the "death" of assimilation, arguing instead for a kind of integration that would allow American black people to merge their double selves into better and truer selves. This merging would allow black Americans to transcend their sense of two-ness, rather than rejecting one or the other of their selves. Thus DuBois calls in this passage for black Americans to become co-workers in a process of integration.

During the Civil Rights Movement, however, much confusion accompanied the term "integration." By the mid-1960s, integration had come to mean the full assimilation of black people into the melting pot of American society so that they would be indistinguishable from other Americans. Understood this way, integration was rejected as a goal by most black people. Some argued for the separation of "black power" as a way of preserving and developing the positive aspects of black American culture and experience, while others attempted to find new ways of expressing the old concept of integration.

Jackson is among those who have sought to advocate integration by simultaneously affirming the (limited) appropriateness of both separatist self-development and assimilationist equal opportunity and full participation, rather than one or the other.[77] Some of this blending of positions comes easily for Jackson, who came to a leadership position in the Civil Rights Movement in the mid-1960s, just as black power advocates such as Stokeley Carmichael of the Student Nonviolent Coordinating Committee (SNCC) were challenging Martin Luther King, Jr., and SCLC about how to characterize the problem of racial justice in America. Jackson, in his own way, has tried to combine both approaches using a variety of images:

> So someone asks, "Reverend, are you against integration?" No, I'm for defining the rules of it. "Reverend, you mean you're against the melting pot?" Yes, I'm against the melting pot; I am for vegetable soup. Melting pot means you pour everything into one and you melt it, and then nothing is nothing and everything is everything. I'm not with that. I'm with the vegetable soup, where you have a common base, but the peas, beans, potatoes, and meat all maintain their identity. When it starts simmering and you start drawing some flavor from the meat, the beans, and the potatoes, then all of us contribute to the base. We contribute to the commonwealth, but we do not lose our identity, our self-control, our self-respect, or our right to self-determination. We don't want a melting pot; we want vegetable soup where we can help determine the worth of our flavor.[78]

He always has insisted on the self-respect of black Americans as the bedrock, the nonnegotiable starting point, of any attempt to achieve racial justice, as this quotation illustrates. Yet he also argues for full participation by black Americans in all aspects of society, for equity and parity.

He combines these two approaches when he calls for full black participation in a new America, not the existing one. A new America, one based on humane values, provides the basis for relativizing the claims of both separation and assimilation. "The renewed focus on racial pride and identity, which we must affirm, is not enough," he maintains. "We must not only be ethnic, we must be ethical and efficient and enduring and excellent."[79] Likewise, full participation alone is not enough: "Black Americans cannot merely fight for full employment because we had full employment during slavery. . . . Full development, not just full employment, must be the ultimate goal."[80] Thus he uses his base in the black community to argue for a fuller and richer society for *all* Americans, not just black Americans.

His use of the language of self-reliance and self-affirmation, associated with separation, and the language of inclusion and full participation, associated with assimilation, is not the result of some inconsistency in him or an attempt to be all things to all people. Instead, it is grounded in the "double consciousness" of the black experience in America. His use of both approaches—and his challenge to go beyond them—grows out of his dual experience of America as being simultaneously a dream and a reality, as described in chapter 2. Jackson's call for "a new America," for going to "higher ground," is his way of calling for an integration that is more than assimilation, for an integration that is a rainbow, a quilt, or vegetable soup rather than a melting pot. This more pluralistic understanding of integration includes aspects of both separation and assimilation but goes far beyond them.

It is his injection of "higher ground" or "vision" into his discussion of social change that makes him a "progressive" rather than just someone advancing his own or his group's interests. Vision and the call to move to higher ground relativize the claims of self-interest and bring about an examination of national purpose. His use of the term "progressive" is not merely his attempt to escape from the problems of being labeled this or that; rather, it is his attempt to challenge both "liberals" and "conservatives" and to stake out an alternative position. Neither "heartless conservatism" nor "boundless liberalism" is the answer, Jackson concludes.[81] Instead, America needs to go "another way," a way based on vision and higher ground. Or, as he has said, "My candidacy represents . . . not just a change in leadership, a new President, but a new direction. We should not get off of a Republican elephant and get on a Democratic donkey that is going in the same direction, only a little slower."[82]

This emphasis on higher ground is his way of calling for funda-mental changes in America; yet because of the particular way he does it, he is calling for fundamental changes that are often in line with the ideals to which Americans typically give lip service, as was discussed in chapter 2. For example, he charges that the Reagan administration "has inverted the basic notions of our Judeo-Christian ethic, encouraging us to beat our plowshares into swords, while we leave the disadvantaged begging for bread."[83]

It is also this emphasis on higher ground that makes many political analysts nervous. Higher ground necessarily deals with ideals, but since political analysts typically recognize self-interest as the only, or at least as the principal, reality, this casts Jackson as an outsider, someone who seems to be playing the game of politics by a different set of rules. He thus is often viewed (1) as a naive idealist who deals only in clichéd generalities and who doesn't understand the realities of rough-and-tumble American politics, (2) as a charlatan who is seeking his own interests under the guise of promoting the common good, or (3) as a dangerous idealogue who is mixing religion and politics.

Some politicians and political analysts view him as a naive idealist, as a man out of his depth, as someone who talks of ideals and speaks only in generalities. For example, the *New Republic* described him in a 1984 editorial as "content with the most vapid of cliches, indifferent to questions of concrete policy."[84] Any examination of his activity, however, will reveal that he routinely, almost compulsively, speaks about the specific events of the day, offering instant commentary, as it were, on questions of concrete policy. His discussion of black economic development, for example (see pp. 45–51 above), involves the general themes of equity and reciprocity, but it also involves attention to concrete details. The moral covenants he has negotiated with businesses include attention to the company's advertising, banking, insurance, legal services, accounting, philanthropy, and purchasing practices as well as to the composition of its general workforce.[85] He uses ideals as his basis for judging current events, as a way of gaining perspective, not as an escape from the specific and concrete. He calls for "realism with high ideals, not idealism without reality."[86] As he says of his own Rainbow Coalition: "We must not measure our own identity by our proximity to the [Democratic party's] campaign. Rather, we must measure [it] by its proximity to our ideals. . . . We must remain consistent with our . . . mission."[87]

Others view him as a charlatan. They believe he is simply using this appeal to America the dream as a way of disguising his true (read: self-) interests. Typical of these observers are Julius Lester, who claimed that Jackson's 1984 presidential campaign was "a race for power (disguised as a presidential campaign),"[88] and William

Safire, who claimed that Jackson "is not running for president of the United States, but is using the campaign for president to run for leadership of blacks in America."[89]

Those who think he really believes what he is saying about the relation of ideals and politics view him as a dangerous idealogue. Some believe that he is trying to use the "moral authority" of the American civil tradition or of the Judeo-Christian biblical traditions to impose his will on others. But this view fails to distinguish between Jackson's approach and those of other politically involved Christian ministers, such as Jerry Falwell or Pat Robertson.[90] Others believe that Jackson is not playing the game of politics by the accepted rules when he speaks of the priority of the "least of these" because he is claiming that some self-interests are more important than others. Mainstream American politicians treat all interests as if they were equivalent. To act otherwise, political theorists argue, is to destroy the possibility of compromise and adjustment, which is essential to democratic politics.[91]

This last charge deserves to be taken up in some detail. He speaks about the priority of the "least of these" and advocates measuring America's greatness by how it treats its young, its old, and its poor. These may appear simply to be rhetorically pleasing ways of advancing one group's interests over another's. This might be the case *if* these groups possessed sufficient political power to advance their own interests effectively. But this is precisely his point: these people are America's disinherited and thus do not enjoy a normal degree of political power. Accordingly, to meet their needs is not so much to prefer one *group* (and its interests) over another as it is to prefer one *kind of values* over another, to prefer "meeting basic human needs" over such values as "private property" or "to the (political) victor go the spoils."[92] He clearly does not think all political interests have equal value. Hence he emphasizes meeting basic human needs, as embodied in the plight of the poor and the powerless: children "in the dawn of life," poor people "in the pit of life," and old people "in the sunset of life."

He frequently refers to "two great traditions: the political and the prophetic" and argues that the "creative tension" between them "makes us healthy, alive, sensitive, alert, and accountable."[93] "Prophets need politicians—they keep reminding us of how things are. Politicians need prophets—they keep reminding us of how things ought to be."[94] In calling for Americans to seek moral higher ground, to go another way, he is attempting to combine both of these traditions.

Calling for moral higher ground is his way of raising substantive questions about individual, group, and national purposes. The more typical view is that national purposes are merely the sum of individuals' or groups' purposes. He, however, believes that national purposes must be consciously addressed; they will not automatically result from individuals and groups seeking their own purposes.

Thus Jackson could declare that it was his 1984 campaign's purpose:

> to transform the quality of American life. We want to restore a moral quality to the political decisions that affect our lives at home and the decisions that affect the lives of our brothers and sisters around the globe. We want to set our nation on a course where the full spiritual, moral, and physical resources of our people can be realized. We want to end the exploitation and oppression of the many by the few.[95]

Without this emphasis on moral higher ground, he would be merely a spokesperson for America's dispossessed. With it, however, he becomes a national leader, both a politician and a prophet, raising fundamental questions about the national interest and national purpose.

6

Jesse Jackson and Controversy

Jesse Jackson is no stranger to controversy. Wherever he goes, controversy seems to follow, and at times, he even seems to invite it. Most people have analyzed the controversy that accompanies him in terms of his personality, its strengths and weaknesses. While there can be no doubt that his personality has been an important ingredient, it is essential not to overlook the essential role that his positions and programs have played in each of these controversial areas.[1] In order to discover why he so often is the focus of controversy, it is necessary to understand his vision for America and his general approach to social and political change.

JACKSON THE OPPORTUNIST

The most general charge against him is that he is an opportunist, utilizing every occasion possible for self-promotion. Consider the following three incidents:

1. On April 4, 1968, Jesse Jackson, along with other staff members of the Southern Christian Leadership Conference (SCLC), was in Memphis, Tennessee, to bolster Martin Luther King, Jr.'s support for striking sanitation workers. Jackson was present at the Lorraine Motel when King was shot. By the time the television cameras arrived half an hour later, Ralph Abernathy was at the hospital, accompanying King's body. Jackson, still on the scene, was interviewed by reporters. Later that same night, he flew home to Chicago

and appeared the next morning on NBC's "Today Show" to discuss King's assassination. Chicago's largely black west side had erupted in flames the night of King's assassination. Mayor Richard J. Daley had ordered police to shoot to kill arsonists and to maim looters. He also called a special meeting of City Council on April 5 to memorialize Dr. King. Jackson attended and attempted to expose the hypocrisy of the Chicago City Council, since just a year and a half earlier they had opposed King's open housing drive there. Wearing the brown turtleneck sweater he had been wearing the day before in Memphis, now smeared with King's blood, Jackson declared: "This blood is on the chest and hands of those who would not have welcomed him here yesterday."[2] As one of his biographers summed it up: "Whether dramatic flair or stage prop, the blood-on-the-shirt motif . . . and the indictments he made to the national TV viewing audience after King's assassination outlined the image he was projecting as a national figure."[3]

2. On December 29, 1983, he led a delegation of fourteen, most of them American religious leaders, to Damascus, Syria, to attempt to negotiate the release of Robert O. Goodman, Jr., a black U.S. navy lieutenant whose plane had been shot down over Syria. His efforts were successful; on January 3, Syrian President Hafez al-Assad released Lt. Goodman to Jackson's delegation. A few days later, President Ronald Reagan honored both Jackson and Goodman at a White House reception, and Jackson took center stage when the TV cameras were present, shifting the spotlight away from the president.

3. In early 1987, a series of racial incidents at the University of Michigan campus in Ann Arbor, coupled with declining black enrollment—down to 5.3 percent from a high of 7.7 percent a decade earlier—culminated in a series of student protests and the occupation of a campus building in late March. Black student leaders invited Jackson to campus. He spoke to a campus rally, met with university president Harold Shapiro, and along with Shapiro announced the university's plans to increase black enrollment and to create a special commission on affirmative action goals and timetables.

These three incidents are representative of the many, many times Jackson has shown up where the television cameras were set up, where he has flown in from out of town to become the spokesperson

100

for local people dealing with a set of problems, where he has stepped into whatever limelight was available. Inarguably, he has mastered the task of getting himself on the television news and saying something memorable or interesting in the thirty seconds available, skills he employed to great advantage during his 1984 presidential campaign, when he did not have the money necessary to run televised commercials and was forced to settle for whatever air time he could command on the news. But it must be noted that this is not a new skill; it is one he has employed for the past score of years.

Incidents such as these raise important questions about his purposes. Is he an opportunistic publicity hound, seeking personal aggrandizement rather than progress on the issues under discussion? During his 1984 presidential campaign, some charged that he was not himself seriously a candidate for the Democratic party's presidential nomination; what he was seeking instead was to be recognized as the president of black America. At the heart of these questions is the issue of authenticity. Are his actions what they appear to be, or is something else going on? Are they "principled" actions or disguised attempts to advance his self-interest? What, really, is his agenda?

The general charge of opportunism often leveled against him includes several distinct elements. Two clusters of these will be examined in some detail. The first cluster revolves around the question of consistency. Some charge that he selects his topics or shifts his principles to suit the particular audience he currently is addressing, that he advocates only what is popular, what a particular audience wants to hear. Second, the charge of opportunism involves the question of motives, that in his various activities he is principally seeking some kind of personal gain rather than progress on the issues he is addressing. This might be personal financial gain, or it might be some other type of personal goal, such as self-aggrandizement. Most specifically, this question of motives has been addressed in terms of whether he might not really be seeking to become "president of black America" or to lay claim to be heir to the mantle of Martin Luther King, Jr. Since Jackson has been a public figure for more than two decades, his record of performance should provide some clues about whether charges such as these are based in reality or are the result of misperceptions.

101

Jackson and Consistency

The charge that he is inconsistent often grows out of the observation that he addresses *so many* specific issues. As a consequence, it is not always clear to everyone why he should be addressing any particular issue—unless it simply is another opportunity to be in the limelight, a charge that is the heart of the second cluster of elements in this general charge of opportunism. Why does he address so many different specific issues? Three aspects of his general approach help explain.

Timeliness. He believes in the importance of being timely, of addressing the issues of the moment. He follows the news very closely and attempts to speak out on events of the day before—rather than after—others do, hoping that his perspective on these events, based on the importance of seeking racial justice, can help shape the contours of public discussion. This is seen most readily by examining his addresses at Operation PUSH over the years. Each Saturday morning for the past twenty years, he has begun his remarks by providing his perspective on the news events—local, national, and international—of the previous week, and his more formal speech that followed rarely failed to address timely topics. Not only were these remarks and speeches broadcast live over local radio stations, but excerpts routinely were picked up and run as news items by the national black radio news networks. In addition, from 1977 to 1983, he had a weekly syndicated newspaper column. It, too, was typically keyed to the events of the day. For example, in January and February of 1980, he commented on racial discrimination in Chicago,[4] affirmative action in higher education,[5] the 1980 presidential campaign,[6] the limits of military power in solving the political problems in Iran and Afghanistan,[7] U.S. policy in the Middle East,[8] and the potential political power of students.[9]

In a sense, this attempt to speak forcefully in a timely way to the issues of the moment is a further instance of the risk taking and bold initiatives which he believes are important to finding solutions to the problems of today's world. Speaking out so quickly on events, however, ensures that he often will be proven wrong by subsequent events. He thus runs the risk of being viewed as merely wanting to hear himself talk. But he believes it is important to act rather than merely react.

Beyond the matter of personal style, however, this attempt to be timely has been incorporated into the institutional approach of first Operation PUSH and then the Rainbow Coalition. Where the executive director of groups such as the National Association for the Advancement of Colored People (NAACP) would be required to get approval from the board of directors before issuing a statement on behalf of the NAACP on a specific public issue, Jackson established an institutional structure where this was not required, a structure in which it was clear that he and he alone was responsible for speaking on behalf of the institution and declaring what it stood for.

Legitimate Range of Competence. With this attempt to be timely, however, he leaves himself open to another charge, namely that he is speaking on issues far beyond the range of his personal and professional competence. Sometimes this is the general charge that, by addressing such a wide range of issues, he lacks focus. No person can speak thoughtfully or knowledgeably about so many issues, the charge goes. This general criticism, however, can be leveled against anyone seeking the presidency, against anyone attempting to speak authoritatively on a wide range of public issues.

But there is a more specific, and more important, version of this charge that he is addressing issues about which he does not legitimately have anything to say.[10] He is, after all, a "black civil rights leader," and what does civil rights have to do with presidential campaigns; the U.S. position regarding Iran, Afghanistan, or the Middle East; or the potential political power of students? How are these "black issues"? Yet he addressed all of these topics in a two-month period in his syndicated newspaper column.

He resists being described as a "black leader," arguing that the intent of such labels is to make him and his message less universal than they are.[11] More than four decades ago, Swedish social scientist Gunnar Myrdal, making the same point, put it this way:

> [The black man] can grow to a degree of distinction, but always as a representative of "his people," not as an ordinary American or an individual in humanity. . . . That is the social role awarded him, and he cannot step out of it. . . . The difference . . . between the Negro and

103

other "racial" minorities—the Jews, for example—is notable. . . . A
Jewish economist is not expected to be a specialist on Jewish labor.
A Jewish sociologist is not assumed to confine himself always to
studying the Ghetto.[12]

Jackson puts the matter directly: "When they refer to us as 'black
leaders,' they are not describing our skin color, . . . they are defining
our domain. . . . When people can define you, they can confine you.
. . . We are not slaves of the ghetto; we are citizens of the world."[13]

For the same reason, he also resists being described as a "civil
rights leader." Those who employ such designations generally want
to limit his legitimacy or his expertise to civil rights issues, narrowly
conceived as dealing with the legal protections and political rights
of citizenship. On the other hand, for the past twenty years, he has
been dealing with racial justice issues, issues which include but are
not limited to civil rights, narrowly conceived. He has been dealing
with those racial justice issues that lie beyond establishing equal
opportunity in the laws; he has been dealing with the economic
aspects of racial justice and with the complex relationship of racial
justice to such areas as education, politics, the mass media, and U.S.
foreign policy.

As noted in chapter 2, his analysis of America's racial situation
provides the starting point and basic frame of reference for his analysis
of all issues. It is an analysis of American society from "a black
perspective—which is the perspective of the rejected."[14] In the more
than three and a half centuries since the first African slaves were
brought to this country in 1619, racial injustice has become so
insinuated in American society that it is difficult to analyze any social
issue and not find racism to be an important component. He not
only sees racial injustice as intertwined with all aspects of American
life, he also sees these aspects of American life as interrelated with
each other. In his view, racial injustice is the number-one threat to
domestic tranquility[15] and is the principal obstacle to creating a new
world order characterized by peace and justice. This is due not only
to the ubiquity of racial injustice in American life but also to what
he calls the "cataracts of race," which keep most Americans from
seeing reality clearly, from seeing the presence of racial injustice in
so many areas of life, and from seeing the interrelation of these areas

of life. Many Americans, white and black, have allowed themselves to be diverted by racial considerations and thus have not sought to find economic and political common ground for addressing the many issues that negatively affect them.

Oddly enough, in a manner that his critics fail to recognize, he actually has confined himself to addressing issues about which he legitimately has something to say. For twenty years Jackson has been addressing racial justice issues. He has been addressing the issues that lie beyond those legal and political rights of citizenship which were directly addressed by the Civil Rights Movement of the 1950s and 1960s, issues that Martin Luther King, Jr., called the "second phase" of the movement for racial justice, namely, the realization of equality.[16] King thought of this second phase as the area of human rights, as distinguished from constitutional (or civil) rights and recognized that this phase was more controversial than the first. "Now we are approaching areas where the voice of the Constitution is not clear. . . . The Constitution assured the right to vote, but there is no such assurance of the right to adequate housing, or the right to an adequate income."[17]

Recognizing the ubiquity of racial injustice in American life is an uncomfortable—even painful—process, even if one's vision were not blurred by racism. The failure by many to recognize the legitimacy of Jackson's addressing the whole range of issues in American life says much more about the perspectives of those questioning his actions than it does about the man himself. As Myrdal pointed out, racial injustice "is an integral part of, or a special phase of, the whole complex of problems in the larger American civilization. It cannot be treated in isolation."[18] Accordingly, he and his research team investigated such diverse areas as migration patterns, agriculture, employment patterns, housing, politics, the police and the courts, churches, education, the press, and even infant-mortality rates. While these areas of life do not seem to be linked to "civil rights," narrowly conceived, they are linked to the larger issue of racial justice. Those who do not see—or do not choose to see—the ubiquitous presence of racial injustice in American life frequently charge Jackson with opportunism. The ingredients involved in making this charge are similar to those involved in attributing the Civil Rights Movement in the South to "outside agitators." A failure to understand American life from the black perspective, from the perspective of the rejected, leads to events which seem to defy conventional explanations. Hence the need for some extraneous cause, such as "outside agitators" or "opportunists."

Consistent Principles.[19] Another aspect of this charge of opportunism is the suspicion that Jackson appeals to one set of principles for making his judgments on one occasion and to another set on another occasion. While no one is—or should be expected to be—fully consistent dealing with a wide range of issues over a period of twenty years, he has been remarkably consistent. The basic principles that inform his positions, as outlined in chapter 5, have been in place during the last twenty years. During this time, he has not significantly altered them.

Looked at this way, it can be said that he has attempted to apply his long-held principles to new issues as they arose. The fact that he addresses such a wide range of timely topics should be seen as his attempt to demonstrate the usefulness and validity of his general perspective on the extent to which racism has affected nearly every aspect of American life.

Others seeing him as an opportunist say that he has tried to be all things to all people, emphasizing one aspect of his perspective to white audiences and another to black ones, allowing each to feel good about what he has to say. If this were so, we would expect Jackson, when dealing with what he calls the "dialectic between effort and opportunity" in bringing about social change, to stress "opportunity" as the key to change to black audiences and "effort" to white ones, in each case making people other than themselves the key to change. Even a cursory examination of his speeches, however, does not substantiate such a suspicion. All of his speeches that involve this dialectic stress that *both* elements are essential, not just one or the other. In fact, to the extent that he does stress one over the other to a particular audience, he stresses the one most likely to challenge that audience out of its complacency and make it uncomfortable. Thus his speeches to largely black groups of high-school students stress the "effort" side of the dialectic, challenging students to take whatever personal responsibility they can for their own education, and his speeches to largely white groups of school administrators stress the "opportunity" side, citing the need to restructure education to create a situation where there can be the opportunity for all students to become educated.[20]

Not only has his position been consistent throughout the years, belying charges of opportunism, but he has shown that he can grow in his understanding of his own principles. "Human rights for all human beings" is one of his principles. This has led him to become a vocal advocate of the Equal Rights Amendment for women and of equal protection under the laws for homosexuals, positions which a decade ago he did not support. He has come to support attempts to add the words "sexual orientation" to Title VII of the 1964 Civil Rights Act (the "National Gay Civil Rights Bill"), and his specification of those groups he wishes to become part of his Rainbow Coalition includes gays and lesbians. Jackson's position on gay and lesbian rights is one which most other candidates considered too politically risky to take in 1984, but he wished to show that he really does believe in human rights for all human beings. This is not the approach of an opportunist.

Thus when the full range of his activities over the past two decades is examined, his practice of speaking out on most public issues becomes evidence not of an opportunism based on shifting or inconsistently applied principles. Instead, it is evidence of his attempts to speak in a timely way to current issues and to call attention to the multitude of ways that racism continues to affect American life.

Public Versus Private Agendas

The second cluster of specific issues involved in the general charge of opportunism often leveled against Jackson revolves around the question of his motives or purposes in his activities. What is his "real" agenda? What is he "really" up to? Does he have one agenda that he publicly pursues but another, private, agenda that is his real agenda?[21] This second cluster of issues is closely related to the first. If he is engaged in issues and activities where he does not seem to belong, then there must be some reason other than those issues to explain his interest in them. He must be up to something else; he must have a private agenda. Thus the interest in what he is getting out of all his activity.

Personal Gain. Even a brief association with him allows one to

107

conclude that he is not interested in living in the lap of luxury. He is a minister (he is co-pastor of Fellowship Missionary Baptist Church in Chicago) and lives in a style consistent with that vocation. He neither drinks nor smokes (and has little tolerance for his staff members who do), and his tastes in food are simple and basic. For entertainment and recreation, he prefers playing basketball in his backyard to having an expensive night out on the town. While in the late 1960s he was noted for having an extensive wardrobe of nontraditional clothing, for the past fifteen years that has been drastically reduced to just a few basic, much more traditional items. He has no interest in fancy cars or exquisite home furnishings.

Nor does he seem interested in financial gain. His salaries at Operation PUSH and at the Rainbow Coalition have been in line with black ministers who pastor large churches, not with physicians, attorneys, or corporate managers. He has not amassed sizable financial holdings. He has owned a home in Chicago for years, and he recently bought one in Washington, D.C. Any charges relating to money leveled against him have had to do with his organization, not with his personal finances. (Tax audits by the IRS have indicated that, as often as not, he has overpaid, not underpaid, his taxes.) But even at PUSH, the charge typically was that money was not being managed well, not that too much was being made. While Operation PUSH has entered into a number of moral covenants involving the economic aspects of racial justice, it has not profited directly from those. For example, one part of the covenant Operation PUSH entered into with Kentucky Fried Chicken in 1982 noted that about 20 percent of KFC's annual $1 million in philanthropy already had been targeted at minority organizations. However, the covenant reads, "the company . . . will explore other opportunities such as research grants to black educational institutions and support of the Martin Luther King, Jr., Center for Nonviolent Social Change."[22] Jackson and Operation PUSH were not targeted to receive anything, and this is true for all the economic covenants he has negotiated. If anything, he and Operation PUSH can be criticized for not being diligent enough in obtaining some clear economic benefit from these covenants.

Most often, however, charges of ulterior motives or personal gain have revolved around assessments of his ego. Rather than some kind of personal financial gain, it is self-aggrandizement, critics charge, that he seeks. His "I am somebody" litany often seems to be as much a self-affirmation as an attempt to get others to break what he calls the dependency syndrome. The spotlight of press attention, critics charge, is the end that he seeks; he is interested in notoriety and in being a celebrity.

Self-Aggrandizement. Inarguably, he has a sizable ego and relishes the attention he now commands. He, however, is operating in arenas where sizable egos are typical, if not essential. First, no one who runs for the presidency can have a small ego. Implicit in being a candidate is the claim that this one person is qualified to lead the most powerful nation in the world and can make a difference. These are not small claims, yet every four years about a dozen people publicly make them. Second, it takes a sizable ego to be a Christian minister, to claim publicly to have been called by God for a special purpose, to claim to be God's spokesperson. Third, it requires a strong ego to stand up to the dehumanizing consequences of American racism. This has been the message he has preached to black Americans for decades, and it is the personal stance he has taken his entire life. Finally, it requires a strong ego to engage in the bold initiatives that so often characterize his activities, such as meeting with Fidel Castro, Yassir Arafat, or Daniel Ortega. It takes no particular gift of insight to realize that these meetings were bound to evoke criticism, if not outrage, from many quarters. Yet he believed these meetings were important, and he was willing to stand alone, if necessary, and be subject to the accompanying criticism.

Acting in these particular public arenas also requires courage. On the most significant level, he has had the courage to act in the face of threats to his life. These threats occur with great regularity, and their number increased to 316 during 1984 when he sought the presidency. The assassinations of Martin Luther King, Jr., and Robert F. Kennedy stand as clear reminders of the reality of the threats Jackson faces daily, given the issues he deals with. He addresses the same issues King addressed, and in addition he has been outspoken about U.S. policies in the Middle East. (Kennedy's assassin, Sirhan Sirhan, apparently was motivated to kill him because of his public positions on the Middle East).[23]

But simply having a large ego and enjoying the limelight are not sufficient grounds for criticism unless they undercut the programmatic goals Jackson seeks. Has he "sold out" on the issues for the sake of personal notoriety? The evidence here is not clear-cut. When negotiating on an issue, he typically presses for broad changes, not just for ones that bring him or his organizations money or publicity. For example, the moral covenant between Operation PUSH and Kentucky Fried Chicken involves changes in ten different areas of corporate operations, including the awarding of franchises, advertising, insurance, legal work, banking, and philanthropy.[24] The focus was broad, not narrow. The covenant was oriented toward long-term social change, not immediate personal publicity, although considerable publicity accompanied the signing of the covenant.

His opponents on a particular issue often have attempted to bring him into line and keep him from criticizing them in public by offering him personal publicity. While he often accepts the publicity, he typically uses the attention to press the issues that animate him— leading to the charge that he is an unpredictable maverick because he does not seem to play by the accepted rules of the game. (See the discussion of this topic, pp. 122–26 below.) For example, prior to the 1984 Democratic National Convention, there was talk that Jackson would be bought off in some way. He responded to that suggestion this way: "I'm not in this mission for private brokering; I am a change agent."[25] And his actions seem to bear this out. At the convention, he was given the time for a major address in prime television viewing time.[26] But that did not keep him from pressing four minority planks before the convention, nor did it keep him from challenging the party and its nominee to provide a "signal" to his constituency to indicate that their needs were being taken seriously.[27] And an examination of his speech to the convention indicates that it was designed to call attention to his constituency and his program, not to himself.

Politician. Roger Wilkins has noted that, when it comes to politics, Jackson is "a natural. He is nourished by the stuff of politics: the issues, the people, the motion, the turmoil, and the thunder."[28] Long before he began running for the presidency, people had recognized that, although he usually identified himself as a minister, Jackson is a deeply political human being. Many Americans hold politicians at arm's length and view them with suspicion. As these people view politicians, their chief motivation appears to be to gain election or reelection, and their positions on issues shift in order to make this possible. Jackson is the object of this same kind of skepticism about his motives and of the suspicion that he is attempting to be all things to all people.

In examining this issue of his agenda, some critics have focused on the conditions of those he calls his "constituency." Have his actions, programs, and speeches bettered the conditions of America's damned, disrespected, and disinherited? If the answer is "no" or "not much," the conclusion these critics, white and black, draw is that Jackson, not his constituency, must be the principal beneficiary of his efforts. As Landess and Quinn ask, "how many people were actually helped by such efforts?"[29] Many have noted that the black middle class has been the principal recipient of the benefits derived from the Civil Rights Movement.[30] It is middle-class blacks who have been in a position to take advantage of the "equal opportunities" won by the Civil Rights Movement. It is also middle-class blacks who have been the principal beneficiaries of Jackson's moral covenants with various businesses. The general condition of the disproportionately large number of black poor people has deteriorated, not become better, in the twenty years he has been in public life.

Few would go as far as Landess and Quinn, who charge:

> If neither the American people nor its president can discern an obvious mandate for "black legislation," it's because Jesse Jackson has not made such a program clear or persuasive. If the nation is muddle-headed and indecisive on matters pertaining to blacks, it's because Jackson has not yet made us understand what it is we are supposed to do.[31]

Yet that is precisely what this kind of thinking can lead to. The issues facing poor black Americans are so large, complicated, and intransigent that only a massive, comprehensive, coordinated campaign can begin to turn them around. The election of black mayors in major cities such as Los Angeles, Chicago, Philadelphia, Detroit, Cleveland, and Atlanta both demonstrates a measure of racial justice already achieved in the political arena and makes possible increased movement toward racial justice in other areas. There is no instance, however, in which the election of a black mayor has *solved* the problems of poor black people in that city. Those who argue that a black mayor should be able to solve these problems usually are thought to possess unrealistic expectations.

The same should be concluded about critics of Jackson who argue that his efforts have done little for poor black people. The problems of poverty and racism require massive, comprehensive, and coordinated national efforts. The last effort of any magnitude was Lyndon B. Johnson's "War on Poverty," which ended twenty years ago. Even that effort, Jackson notes, was feeble and half-hearted when judged by the size of the problems themselves.[32] Since that time, the federal government has retreated from these issues, exacerbating rather than ameliorating these problems. Thus if Jackson is open to criticism because the plight of the black poor in America has worsened in the past score of years, so are all other black leaders, be they mayors, members of Congress, or leaders in the NAACP, the National Urban League, or SCLC.

What Jackson has been doing, above all, these past twenty years has been trying to keep the issue of racial justice before the American public, raising it as an issue when it was not popular, when people did not wish to see it. His aphorism aimed at students—"If your mind can conceive it and your heart can believe it, you can achieve it"[33]—embodies some fundamental elements in his approach to racial justice and social change. "If your mind can conceive it . . .": Imagination and being able to see issues clearly must come first. Americans cannot act to promote racial justice until they first see the presence and extent of racial injustice. ". . . if your heart can believe it . . .": Once social issues are recognized, the matter of will becomes crucial. That is why he stresses the matter of priorities as the key political question. ". . . you can achieve it": In his approach, achievement comes at the end of a complex process. Unfortunately, for the sake of racial justice in America, he has been forced by the general conditions in society to deal mainly with the earlier steps in the process leading to achievement.

All in all, it can be concluded that ego satisfaction, or what some have called Jackson's "drive to excel"[34] or his inner drive to be number one, is a reasonable candidate for the "ulterior motive" in much that he does. He clearly accepts the spotlight when it is offered (and often seeks it when it is not offered). The key question is whether he allows his own ego needs to get in the way of progress on the issues he addresses.

"President of Black America." A very focused way of raising this general question of what he "really" is seeking is the question of whether he is seeking to become "president of black America." While this was raised as an issue during his 1984 presidential campaign,[35] this issue is not new. In the early 1960s, Martin Luther King, Jr., was recognized by the news media and by most white politicians as *the* black leader or as the focus of the Civil Rights Movement. Such recognition, however, was not uncontested and was controversial. Following his assassination in 1968, there was a scramble to identify his "successor." Even though Ralph Abernathy was King's organizational successor as head of SCLC, he never was regarded as King's successor in being *the* black leader. Early on, Jackson was among those named as a possibility. When *Time* magazine devoted a special issue to "Black America 1970," it chose to run the cover story on Jackson, although the story was entitled, "Jesse Jackson: One Leader Among Many."[36] Six months earlier, a *Playboy* interviewer had proclaimed Jackson "the fiery heir apparent to Martin Luther King."[37]

To be sure, Jackson was a member of SCLC's staff (as were others, such as Andrew Young) and was national director of Operation Breadbasket, SCLC's arm seeking racial justice in the economic arena. Thus there were direct organizational, institutional ties between Jackson and King. Over the years, Jackson has encouraged people to identify him with King. In his speeches, he often refers to himself as King's disciple. Although he broke organizational ties with SCLC in 1971 and formed his own Operation PUSH, the PUSH headquarters building in Chicago is called "Dr. King's Workshop," and paintings of King are scattered throughout the building, some having Jackson present along with King. Most controversial, of course, are his appearances on TV and at the Chicago City Council meeting following King's assassination. In short, it is not difficult to identify numerous ways in which Jackson, either boldly or more subtly, has claimed to be the heir to the mantle of Martin Luther King, Jr.

Do these claims stand up under scrutiny? On the organizational level, there is no doubt that King himself designated Ralph Abernathy to be his successor at SCLC. Judged in this way, any claim Jackson may have to be the heir to King's mantle seems spurious. Only Abernathy, and perhaps Andrew Young, legitimately could make such a claim.

But there are two additional aspects to this claim to be heir to King's mantle. First, King was a charismatic leader, and such leadership is not acquired by being elected or appointed to certain offices within an organization, Such leadership, instead, exists when others recognize it and believe it to be legitimate. This is why Ralph Abernathy never was regarded as *the* black leader in the United States the way King was, although he was King's long-time friend and was his successor as president of SCLC.

Following King's assassination, no one immediately succeeded him as the recognized leader of black Americans, as *Time* magazine recognized in its cover story on Jackson in 1970. Since then, there have been numerous efforts by the news media to identify such a leader, and several persons have vied for the privilege of being so identified. By the early 1980s, Jackson had been recognized by black Americans, if not yet by the news media and white politicians, as filling this role, if, indeed, anyone did. Each year since 1981 he has been among the "ten men most admired by Americans," as determined by annual Gallup polls, and within the black community, his standing has been even better. *Ebony* magazine readers in 1980 named him the "living black man who has done the most to advance the cause of black Americans" during the thirty-five years since *Ebony*'s founding in 1945.[38] During 1980, four separate polls were taken of black Americans, asking which black leader was "most popular," "most effective," "most admired," or "most influential." He placed first in three of these, finishing second to Andrew Young in the fourth poll.[39] In mid-1981, *Ebony* magazine called Jackson "perhaps the most charismatic, most outspoken, most combative, most visible and, alas, most controversial black leader on the civil and human rights front."[40] Thus charges during his 1984 campaign that he was *seeking to become* president of black America were misplaced since that was a role he had been playing for some time. It was not something he had to seek in 1984.

114

Second, being heir to Martin Luther King, Jr.'s mantle also means being faithful to the principles that informed King and to the issues he pursued. As outlined toward the end of chapter 1, King, at the end of his life, was addressing racial injustice in its many dimensions and manifestations, not just laws that were barriers to equal opportunity. In particular, he had begun addressing the economic and political manifestations of racial injustice. He also was seeking to discover nonviolent tactics to employ beyond the mass nonviolent action which had characterized the Civil Rights Movement.

> The notion that ethical appeals and persuasion alone will bring about justice [is fallacious]. This does not mean that ethical appeals must not be made. It simply means that those appeals must be undergirded by some form of constructive coercive power. . . . Mass nonviolent demonstrations will not be enough. . . . To produce change, people must be organized to work together in units of power. These units may be political, . . . they may be economic.[41]

King also had begun addressing the ways the triple evils of racism, poverty, and militarism reinforced each other in America:

> In the days ahead we must not consider it unpatriotic to raise certain basic questions about our national character. We must begin to ask, "Why are there forty million poor people in a nation overflowing with such unbelievable affluence?" Why has our nation placed itself in the position of being God's military agent on earth, and intervened recklessly in Vietnam and the Dominican Republic? Why have we substituted the arrogant undertaking of policing the whole world for the high task of putting our own house in order?
>
> All these questions remind us that there is a need for a radical restructuring of the architecture of American society. For its very survival's sake, America must reexamine old presuppositions and release itself from many things that for centuries have been held sacred. For the evils of racism, poverty, and militarism to die, a new set of values must be born.[42]

Jesse Jackson, along with many others, clearly has dedicated his life to addressing racial injustice, especially in its economic and political manifestations, to organizing political and economic "units of power" to produce change. Unlike most others, however, he has pursued racial justice through institutions for which that was the principal focus. First Operation Breadbasket and then Operation

PUSH had the economic dimension of racial injustice as their principal focus. His Rainbow Coalition seeks to overcome some of the political manifestations of racial injustice. Most often, those pursuing racial justice have worked through other institutions—most notably the churches, politics, and educational institutions—all institutions whose primary focus necessarily is on something other than racial justice. Racial justice, then, becomes a secondary rather than a primary concern of these institutions.

Throughout his public career, Jackson, following in the footsteps of King, consistently has addressed the triple evils of racism, poverty, and militarism. Like King, he is a minister who has considered himself a spokesperson for America's dispossessed, particularly black Americans and poor people, and he has sought to pressure businesses, labor unions, educational systems and institutions, and governmental agencies at all levels to first recognize and then deal constructively with racism, poverty, and militarism. In so doing, he lays legitimate claim to be among the principal heirs to the mantle of Dr. Martin Luther King, Jr.

How, then, are we to understand the persistent charges of opportunism leveled at him? On the one hand, it must be concluded that Jackson is a highly motivated, highly political person with a sizable ego who almost instinctively moves toward the limelight. On the other hand, he has been a consistent, persistent advocate of racial justice in all its dimensions.

Given the pervasiveness of racial injustice in American life and the way most Americans have come to equate racial justice with "civil rights," narrowly conceived, most people are likely to miss the connections between the apparently diverse issues Jackson addresses or to see why he should be addressing them at all. Given the fact that he is a highly political person who has chosen to enter the realm of electoral politics, he is likely to be viewed with suspicion by those who are skeptical of politicians. Thus—even without the additional, and highly significant, element of his ego and its needs—he is operating in an arena and in a manner in which anyone likely would be viewed with suspicion and charged with being an opportunist. The situation itself is structured this way. The fact that he seems driven to be number one simply adds fuel to this charge.

JACKSON AND JEWS

Early in his 1984 campaign for the presidency, Jackson had a private, off-the-record conversation with Milton Coleman, a black reporter for the *Washington Post,* in which he at one point referred to Jews as "Hymies" and to New York City as "Hymietown." Sometime later in mid-February, Coleman decided to put this private, off-the-record conversation on the record and included it at the end of a long story. Initially, Jackson neither confirmed nor denied making the comments. A week later, in a sermon delivered at Temple Adath Yeshurun in Manchester, N.H., he admitted making the remarks and apologized.[43]

But the controversy did not end there. Among his most visible supporters in 1984 was Louis Farrakhan, leader of the Nation of Islam. Farrakhan was among the American religious leaders who had accompanied Jackson on his trip to Syria earlier in 1984 to obtain the release of the downed navy flier Lt. Robert Goodman. A month after the public stir over Jackson's "Hymie" remarks, Farrakhan publicly denounced Milton Coleman, the reporter who made the remarks public, calling him a "Judas and an Uncle Tom" and issuing a vague death threat. Charges and countercharges flew back and forth between Farrakhan and leaders of various Jewish groups. In one exchange Farrakhan referred to Judaism as a "gutter religion." Jackson was called upon to renounce Farrakhan and his support because of Farrakhan's anti-Semitism. Jackson repudiated Farrakhan's remarks, calling them "reprehensible and morally indefensible" and said "such statements have no place in my own thinking or in this campaign."[44] Jackson also apologized for the entire controversy on several occasions, including his nationally televised address to the Democratic National Convention in July. But while denouncing Farrakhan's anti-Semitic remarks, he never repudiated Farrakhan as a person.

Without a doubt, this complex of events in Jackson's 1984 campaign provoked the most controversy about his candidacy. It also raised serious questions about his personal integrity and the integrity of his call for people to "leave racial battleground, come to common economic ground, and rise to higher moral ground."

In what context should these events be viewed? What standards of judgment should be employed? At the time, he himself suggested three contexts:[45] (1) He pointed to broader tensions that had arisen in recent years between blacks and Jews. (2) He admitted that at times there can be some distance between the ideals one affirms and aspires to and the lived realities of everyday life. He was a fallible human being and was willing to be judged by the ideals he affirmed. (3) He argued that his statements should be judged in the larger context of his public career.

1. As many have pointed out, the tension between blacks and Jews already existed when he uttered his "Hymie" remarks. Although many have pointed to his 1979 trip to the Middle East in which he was photographed hugging Yassir Arafat as the event that created bad relations between blacks and Jews, the tension between these two groups is more broadly based than this and existed long before 1979. Adolph L. Reed, Jr., presents much of this ably in "Blacks and Jews in the Democratic Coalition," a chapter in his book, *The Jesse Jackson Phenomenon*.[46] He argues that "neither Jackson's offensive remarks nor his association with a critical posture toward Israel can account for the intensity of Jewish elites' reactions and the proliferation of accusations of black anti-Semitism. Similar moral slurs by others [who were white] . . . have failed to elicit comparably strident reactions."[47] Black/Jewish conflict over the past two decades, Reed claims, is based on a "hidden agenda," which he identifies as "material interest."[48] "The fight against discrimination in higher education, restricted housing covenants, and the like aided Jews as much as blacks,"[49] Reed observes, but the same has not been true of affirmative action strategies. "Those strategies are understood by Jewish elites as infringements on norms for allocation of privilege from which they benefit and which they interpret as rights. This, then, is the substantive basis of black/Jewish conflict in the current period."[50] Accordingly, Reed notes that "the anti-Jackson diatribe was expressed consistently on three levels: two emotional and hysterical, one calm and programmatic"[51]—(1) Jackson's "Hymie" remarks and his link to Louis Farrakhan; (2) his association with Yassir Arafat and Jackson's criticism of Israel (in a context in which either was viewed by many Jews as conclusive evidence of anti-

Semitism;[52] and (3) his advocacy of affirmative action. "The three were tied together neatly, and," Reed concludes, "it was the last that was the substantive issue."[53]

2. In his response to this incident, Jackson repeatedly noted that he was "a public servant, not a perfect servant."[54] Even though he speaks of the importance of moral leadership in politics, he does not claim always to be above reproach. "None of us," he said, "has achieved perfection and none is beyond redemption."[55] Accordingly, he offered public apologies on several well-publicized occasions, including his nationally televised speech to the Democratic party's 1984 national convention.[56] Thus he articulated standards by which he himself was willing to be judged and to which he did not always live up.

3. He also suggested that his actions over his entire public career and especially that his policy proposals ought to be examined to see if they were anti-Semitic. In his initial speech on this matter, he recited part of his own public activities opposing anti-Semitism. His position on the conflict in the Middle East is that the United States should "use its diplomatic and economic strength to reconcile both [Israel and the Palestinians] so that the cycle of pain can end."[57]

In the most extensive investigation to date of Jackson's position on the Middle East, David A. Coolidge, Jr., examines three groups of theories that have been used to explain Jackson's position: personal explanations, ideological explanations, and moral explanations.[58] Coolidge notes that theories "which attribute Jackson's position primarily to his personality by and large . . . begin with the assumption that his position is wrong, and proceed from there to offer various psychological reasons for why he allegedly went astray."[59] "It is not worth arguing that Jesse Jackson is especially sensitive to Jewish concerns, or that he is not ambitious, or that he does not have a stubborn streak," Coolidge observes. These all may be true, but "as explanations of his position, however, the observations are inadequate. On the whole, they only confirm the comment of Cornel West that 'the label of anti-Semitism attaches very readily to anyone seriously critical of Israel.' "[60] Coolidge then examines the attempts to explain Jackson's position in terms of "his ideological affinity with movements of oppressed people in the Third World," an approach that, he observes, "at least has the merit of being advanced by his supporters as well as his detractors."[61] After examining the evidence, he concludes that "Jackson continually frustrates those who comfortably divide the world into 'good guys' and 'bad guys.' "[62] In short, Jackson is more of a pragmatist than an ideologue. Instead Coolidge claims that Jackson's approach has "a three-step moral structure": (a) assertion, which flows out of a self-respect rooted in all human beings being children of God, (b) recognition, which affirms the selfhood of others, including one's opponents, and (c) cooperation.[63] Coolidge finds Jackson's approach rooted in the teaching of the black church and concludes: "It appears to be a positive approach to conflict which recognizes the humanity of all parties without lessening the struggle for 'a just society and a peaceful world.' "[64]

Beyond these three contexts for judging the "Hymie" incident which Jackson explicitly suggested at the time are two others which should be considered: (4) the hypocrisy of most white Americans on the issues of racial justice and discrimination; and (5) the general moral tone of a candidate and a candidacy.

4. Following the "Hymie" incident and then Louis Farrakhan's statements, many black leaders, including Jackson, took note of several things. One was that Jackson and others were being asked to denounce not only what Farrakhan had said but also to renounce him as a person. Virtually every black leader refused to do this, and all bristled at the suggestion that this was what was called for. Farrakhan, as Robert Michael Franklin has pointed out perceptively, has taken on the role of "black America's prosecuting attorney, . . . forcefully pointing out discrepancies between American political rhetoric and the reality of black American life."[65] Most black Americans recognize the validity of most of what Farrakhan says. Further, the mainstream news media seemed to establish the renunciation of Farrakhan as the litmus test for considering someone a responsible, legitimate black leader. A person's track record did not matter; only this one test counted. And, hypocritically, no similar test was created for white politicians on the issue of racial justice. It was Jesse Jackson, not the white news media, who confronted Ronald Reagan in Chicago on August 5, 1980, about the overt

support Reagan was receiving from the Ku Klux Klan. It was Jackson and other (mainly black) leaders, not the news media, who continually had to bring up Reagan's regressive approach to racial justice issues, such as his court appointments, his support for the minority white South African government, his opposition to the extension of the Voting Rights Act, and his opposition to all forms of affirmative action. Reagan's anti-racial-justice policies were no secret; it is this— and not some blind loyalty to the Democratic party—that accounted for more than 90 percent of black voters in 1980 and again in 1984 opposing Reagan at the polls. Although black people were well aware of Reagan's dismal record on racial justice, he rarely had to answer to the news media for it.

5. After Gary Hart's withdrawal from the 1988 presidential race in May of 1987 following allegations of romantic liaisons with a young woman, Jackson addressed the "moral issue" involved. He noted that his own campaign had always attempted to address moral issues. Then, while not denying that extramarital sexual relationships were moral issues, he encouraged people not to equate morality with sexuality, because morality is much broader than that. "Our illicit relationship with South Africa . . . is a moral issue, too," he argued, and our government's support of "the contras in Central America, that is a moral issue, too. . . . Let's not limit moral tone [to sexuality]." We must, he said, have "a broader perspective on the whole question of moral tone."[66] Noting the post-mortem revelations of the extramarital sexual relationships of such presidents as Thomas Jefferson, Dwight Eisenhower, and John Kennedy, Jackson concluded: "I am glad that we did not lose their public service on that issue alone."[67] So he argued that sexual morality should be placed in the perspective of morality more broadly considered.

Similarly, we might inquire about the relationship of his "Hymie" remarks to morality, broadly conceived, to the broad issue of racial justice, or to the goal of establishing a "just society and a peaceful world." So considered, his remarks certainly undercut his own political agenda of creating a rainbow coalition. In his apologies, however, he showed that he was willing to hold himself to the same standards he articulated for others. When viewed in the contexts of his entire public career and of his political positions, these remarks only subtract and detract from his emphasis on the moral dimensions of political issues and show him to be a fallible human being; they do not negate his insistence that, at base, political issues are moral issues.

JACKSON AS MAVERICK

In the summer of 1984, following all the primary elections held by the Democratic party to select delegates to its national convention, where its nominee for president would be named, it was clear that Walter Mondale had enough delegates to win the nomination and that neither Jackson nor Gary Hart, singly or combined, had enough delegates to stop him. Journalists and politicians wondered aloud whether Jackson would bolt the party and run as a third-party candidate. Would he support the party's platform and its nominee? Would he agree to play the game of politics by the generally accepted "rules," or was he an incurable maverick? He encouraged such speculation by indicating that he and the constituency he represented were looking for a "signal" that they and their interests were being taken seriously. Only after such a signal had been given could he support the party's nominee and platform.

Most press accounts treated this as if it were a stance Jackson had created for this particular situation, in part out of frustration, in part because he was a political novice, and in part as a means to gain personal publicity. An examination of his career and his general approach to public issues, however, reveals that this approach—far from being unique to this occasion—is one he typically has employed and regularly has been criticized for. Most often, his reputation as a political maverick has been explained in terms of his personality. But the activities which people cite to brand him a maverick are not adequately explained by his personal political frustrations or by his personality, however apparent these may be, but by his approach to politics and by certain political judgments that he makes.

More explicitly than most politicians, he is an advocate of coalition politics, as the name of his own organization, the Rainbow Coalition, indicates. An examination of his approach to coalitions shows that the questions the press typically raised in the summer of 1984 about whether Jackson would bolt the party and run as an independent were misplaced and misfocused, centering around him as a person and the accepted "rules of the game." More appropriate would have been questions about the conditions under which he might bolt the Democratic party, questions about what the party owed him and his constituents, questions about how the political "rules of the game" typically have affected voters in his Rainbow Coalition, and questions about how his constituency might be important to the November election, even though he did not have the delegates to block Mondale's nomination.

Three concepts are crucial to Jackson's understanding of political coalitions: interests, reciprocity, and leverage. During the first half of 1978, he addressed both the Republican National Committee[68] and the liberal Americans for Democratic Action[69] and presented his basic approach to politics. In these speeches, as elsewhere, he argues that self-interest is the basis for all political organizing and that coalitions are based upon shared self-interests or mutual needs.[70] The first step in political organizing, then, is to determine what the interests are, to raise them to the level of self-consciousness so they can be pursued. While this step is clear to politicians and analysts, it typically has not been clear to his constituency of "the damned, the disinherited, the disrespected, and the despised."[71] Were this step clearer to his constituency, these people, Jackson argues, would not be in this condition. If they recognized their own interests and effectively pursued them in the political arena, he argues, they could not be disrespected and disinherited because there are so many voters and potential voters who fall into these categories. This is, in large part, what he means by "the old minorities constitute the new majority." But these "old minorities" by no means have identical interests. The political power of these disinherited groups, therefore, depends upon their ability to recognize common interests they may have and to organize coalitions based on their mutual needs.

Why has this not happened before? He argues that the politicians currently in power do not find it in their own interests to encourage disinherited groups to seek their interests because these politicians' power has been won by dealing with the interests of other, usually wealthier, groups. Thus the disinherited must look to themselves for political empowerment, not to someone already in power. This is what he means by his oft-repeated phrase, "Nobody will save us for us but us." He argues that to expect change to come "from the top down is a false expectation. . . . It is unrealistic to think that the slavemaster will voluntarily bring an end to slavery. Freedom does not come from the Big House or the White House but from your house and my house."[72]

Further, politicians often have used race to obscure the interests of the disinherited. Consequently, disinherited groups often have found themselves mired in "racial battlegrounds." Instead, they must search for "economic common ground." As Jackson argued to the Alabama state legislature in 1983:

> As leaders, we must remove the cataracts of race from the eyes of our people and lift them out of poverty, ignorance, disease, and fear. . . . If our people can learn to play together on the ball field and die together on the battlefield, then we can teach them the value of turning to each other to improve their economic and social conditions, rather than turning on each other in racial . . . hostility.[73]

Second, coalition politics involves reciprocity. While self-interest is the starting point for building a coalition, coalitions necessarily involve recognizing the interests of all the groups in the coalition. Within a coalition, then, he argues, there must be a relationship of reciprocity rather than of domination. No group's support should be taken for granted, and no group's interests should be ignored. The actual situation for black Americans, however, has been very different from this. Following the 1984 Democratic party's national convention, he observed:

> The Democratic coalition—workers and labor, women, blacks, Hispanics, Jews, and youth—came together last week. But for blacks and Hispanics, there is a gap between our joint mission and the party's message. . . . The black and Hispanic sector of the coalition is expected to deliver thirty percent of the national vote. But the absence of blacks and Hispanics in the administration, structure, public policy, and direction-giving positions in the campaign . . . has created extreme rage and anger in the black and Hispanic communities. . . . The assumption continues to be that the Republicans will still write us off and the Democrats can still take us for granted.[74]

On another occasion, he observed: "Blacks and Hispanics have consistently voted for white candidates. We have been the most loyal members of the Democratic party. . . . The Democratic party must learn the lesson of reciprocal voting—if blacks and Hispanics vote for whites, then whites must vote for blacks and Hispanics."[75] Accordingly, he has argued, "Black people must pursue a strategy that prohibits one party or one element within a party from taking us for granted or another party or element from writing us off."[76]

Third, his approach to coalition politics involves the concept of leverage. He thinks of power as "the ability to achieve purpose."[77] Leverage involves using whatever power a person or group may have to the best advantage possible, especially when that power is not sufficient to achieve the desired outcome on its own. Leverage typically is used to affect where the balance of power will lie. In the political arena, he argues that black voters

> can adopt a strategy where we give all of our votes to one group of people based on blind loyalty rather than vested interest and reciprocity. . . . I can't endorse this strategy . . . because it gives us power but no leverage. A football team that runs *all* its plays on the ground and never throws a pass can be defensed and stopped. . . . We've got to diversify our game plan . . . [and] exercise all our political options based on vested interest and reciprocity.[78]

Jackson believes black Americans and others of his constituency of the damned, the disinherited, the disrespected, and the despised have been in a political situation in which one political party, the Republican, has ignored them and the other, the Democratic, has taken them for granted. In this situation, he calls for his Rainbow Coalition to become a "third force" in American politics, pressuring Republicans from the outside and Democrats from the inside, as a way to have their interests taken seriously and as a way of moving the American political agenda beyond various groups' interests to a consideration of the common good.[79]

Viewed in this light, all the speculation about whether he would bolt the Democratic party and run as an independent could have been answered by asking whether the interests of his constituency were being addressed by the Democratic party's nominee and platform, whether members of his Rainbow Coalition were being integrated into the party's national campaign, whether members of the Rainbow Coalition who were running for local and state-level offices were receiving strong backing from the Democratic party, and by asking Jackson how he thought he could gain maximum leverage for his positions—operating within the Democratic party or running as an independent. If none of these issues was addressed, however, he and his constituents would have found themselves pushed out of the party. Thus movement toward a third party, if it were to come, would have been initiated by those already in power within the Democratic party—not by Jackson.

While it is true that he is much better at being the focal point of a coalition than at simply being one of its members (thereby reinforcing his image as a maverick), his aloofness cannot be explained by personality alone. Much more important is his view of the political process, how blacks and others have not fared well under the existing "rules of the game," and how change for the better might be brought about.

CONTROVERSY AS EDUCATION

Not all of the controversy surrounding Jesse Jackson is a result of misperception or misunderstanding, however. He deliberately creates some of it for the sake of educating people. He described the rationale for this approach in a speech entitled "Politics as an Educational Forum":

> Education . . . cannot be left solely to professional educators, for they cannot do the job alone. The public schools should lay an educational foundation—that is, teach basic skills, provide background and a knowledge base, help to develop and refine the thinking and rational processes. But education must never be totally disconnected from the issues of the day. . . . After all, it was Dr. Martin Luther King, Jr., leading a boycott of a bus company in Montgomery, Alabama, that educated the nation to the evils of apartheid in 1956. It was students involved in "Freedom Rides" that educated the nation to the violence which undergirded and was inherent in enforcing apartheid. It was children marching in Selma, Alabama, that educated the nation to the denial of voting rights for all American citizens. It was students, clergy, and people of conscience leading marches, teach-ins, and other forms of drama that educated the nation to the evil in which our nation was involved in Vietnam. . . . Even today, nonviolent civil disobedience

by those opposed to the use of nuclear weapons is helping to educate and increase the consciousness of the masses of the American people relative to the dangers of a nuclear holocaust. . . . There are broader platforms of education than just the classroom.[80]

Many of his controversial activities, then, must be seen as attempts to educate the American public about current conditions and issues, as attempts to change the focus of current discussions, and as attempts to provide more policy options when the choices are too narrow. He reminds us that most of the civil rights marches were for the purpose of educating people, and most of his public activities with Operation PUSH and with the Rainbow Coalition should be viewed in this light. For example, in the midst of the farm crisis in January of 1985, he organized an informal "farmers' market" at Operation PUSH headquarters in Chicago. Farmers brought in truckloads of produce and sold directly to city dwellers at prices above those the farmers usually received and well below those the city residents usually paid. Jackson hoped to teach city folk about the existence of the farm crisis and farmers about the importance to their own economic well-being of those living in urban areas. He noted the important link between "the rural feeders" and "the urban eaters." Government programs such as food stamps or the Women, Infants, and Children (WIC) program assist not only the recipients, who usually are urban, but also farmers. In addition, these programs affect grocery stores and all the "middle men" in the food production and distribution chain.

As part of Operation PUSH's fourteenth annual convention, held in Memphis, Jackson organized an expedition to Tunica, Mississippi, located just thirty miles south of Memphis. In his convention address, he then observed:

> President Reagan's "safety net" has a gaping hole in it. Tunica, Mississippi, is the most graphic example of the government's inaction, its wrong direction, and a failed public policy relative to the poor. Tunica, Mississippi, just thirty miles south of Memphis on highway 61, is the poorest county in America. The county has 9,600 residents, including 1,300 in the city of Tunica. The county is 75 percent black and 25 percent white. The city is 75 percent white and 25 percent black. Sugar Ditch is located in Tunica. Sugar Ditch is a group of shanties housing about two hundred poor people, mostly women and

children, located between a new downtown business district and $50,000–$100,000 homes. Thirty-eight millionaires live in Tunica. Rich farmers are paid not to farm, while the average per capita yearly income in Tunica is around $4,000. There is no indoor plumbing in Sugar Ditch. Feces and other waste matter are thrown into an open ditch—their sewer—just five to seven feet from the houses where children eat, sleep, and play. One mother testified that roaches and other rodents eat as many potatoes as her children. I saw thousands and thousands of roaches in the houses and on the food with my own eyes. The tax assessor and two city council members own property in Sugar Ditch. Residents pay between $25 and $85 a month to live there. They are charged for sewer services they never receive.

Five state health agencies are charged with the responsibility of protecting the health and safety of its citizens. Yet never has there been a formal investigation into the health conditions or status of Tunica or Sugar Ditch residents. The public school has 2,064 students, less than twenty of them white. The white children go to an all-white, private, Christian, segregated academy called the Tunica Institute of Learning. Public officials divert funds for the public school to the private school. The public school has a chemistry *room* but no equipment or chemicals. Tunica County has the highest rate of substandard or deteriorated housing of the 82 counties in Mississippi, the poorest state in the union.

The health, housing, and educational atrocities are the *effects*. The *cause* is a morally bankrupt political order and unenforced laws. Tunica has five city council members, all elected at-large, thus all-white, in a city that is 25 percent black. The governor is willing to provide trailers for the residents of Sugar Ditch, but the city says that they have no property *within the city* on which to put them. The trailers can only be put in the county. Thus the residents of Sugar Ditch are being forced to choose between housing and dignity and the right to vote.

Blacks, although a vast majority in the county, live mainly on plantations. The plantation owners join together to block new industry and new jobs from coming to Tunica in order to preserve their cheap seasonal labor.

Thus, politically, urban blacks are disenfranchised and left powerless through at-large election and dual registration schemes. Never in the history of the city of Tunica has a black been elected or appointed to any public office. Rural blacks are disenfranchised and left powerless because of economic intimidation on the plantation and the lack of job alternatives beyond the plantation. Blacks are 40 percent of Mississippi's population, therefore a potentially potent political force. There is a conspiracy in Mississippi to leave blacks uneducated, with poor health care, few jobs or job training, and politically disenfranchised so they will leave the state—and leave the power in the hands of a white power elite. The people of Tunica are being held hostage to poverty and are being forced to live in a permanent state of institutionalized terror. . . . The welcoming format of the Statue of Liberty and the tall buildings of Manhattan are good for television, but they do not represent reality to most Americans.[81]

In early May of 1985, Western European countries organized a series of events to celebrate the fortieth anniversary of the end of World War II in Europe. As part of this, President Ronald Reagan spoke to the European Parliament and also made a controversial visit to the graves of S.S. troops at a cemetery in Bitburg, Germany. Jackson scheduled a visit to Western Europe at this same time, also addressed the European Parliament, and was the principal speaker at a major peace rally in West Berlin. While Reagan was visiting the Bitburg cemetery, Jackson visited the site of a former Nazi concentration camp. In his speech to the peace rally, Jackson wanted Europeans to know that there was an American alternative to the policies of Ronald Reagan. He also wanted Europeans to address the problems of the 1980s rather than simply to celebrate the victories of the 1940s.

Today, forty years later, May 8, 1985, the scene of desecration and death is before us. Today the source and scope of death in this war make us tremble. . . . The scenes of historical shame stand as landmarks that should remind us of humankind's low moments. . . . We must never forget nor remove these ancient landmarks—the places where the victims lost their lives, the victimizers lost their souls, and a nation lost its innocence in the government conspiracy to exterminate a people. . . . We must remember lest we forget. . . . This generation cannot resurrect the dead of 1945, but it can save the living of 1985. We must roll the stone away and go forward. . . . This day we must choose another course that the human race might be spared this nightmare again. Yesterday it was Nazism and slave camps. Today it is apartheid in South Africa and missile deployment in Europe that reduce the planet to a death camp.[82]

These examples show clearly the educational purpose of many of Jackson's activities. Critics often have claimed that his activities are "merely symbolic" and lack substance. This charge certainly has been made about his presidential campaigning. In a sense, these critics are correct: the activities *were* symbolic. But they were not "merely symbolic," meaning futile. Rather, they were symbolic activities undertaken for the purpose of educating people to the conditions of American life, particularly in terms of racial injustice or the ways in which the "cataracts of race" have kept Americans from seeing the nature of other problems.

This chapter has examined four general areas of controversy: Jackson as opportunist, Jackson and Jews, Jackson as maverick, and controversy as education. Understanding his personality may be of some help in understanding each of these areas of controversy. However, if one wants to discern why he does what he does, it is absolutely essential to understand his basic ideas, his belief in the importance of analyzing American life from the perspective of the rejected, and his understanding of how social change occurs. Once these elements are understood, it is possible to see connections between his various activities and statements. His ideas and activities have been consistent during his twenty years of public life. Given who Jackson is (an intelligent, aggressive, highly motivated black man), what his agenda has been (to deal with the aspects of racial justice that lie beyond establishing equal opportunity), and the general climate in American society during the past twenty years (shrinking from any engagement with the complex issue of racial justice beyond passing laws that provide for equal opportunity)—it is not surprising that he and his activities have been controversial. In fact, it would be surprising if they were not.

Epilogue

In this book, I have attempted to demonstrate that understanding Jesse Jackson and his work requires a careful examination of the shape and development of his ideas. I believe three elements are of fundamental importance:

1. Racism as his main interpretive principle. Jackson views America from a black perspective, which he describes as "the perspective of the rejected." His understanding of America's racism—and, by extension, rejection in all its forms—serves as the basis for his analysis of all other issues in American life. Knowing this helps make sense, for example, of his dual approach to America: as a dream of hope and as a negative reality.

2. The dialectic between effort and opportunity. This interrelation between changed hearts—be they individuals or nations—and changed institutions means that, while change can begin at either point, it must include both elements if it is to be complete and lasting.

3. His threefold view of the nature of reality: (a) the worth of each individual, (b) the interrelation and interdependence of people and, indeed, of all reality, and (c) the importance of vision for human fulfillment. For Jackson, each of these depends, ultimately, on belief in a God of justice. Out of this grows his confidence that human activity can make a difference. Accordingly, he defines "sin" not as hubris (an enlarged sense of self) but as apathy.

As I have been working on this project, many people have inquired, What do you *really* think about Jesse Jackson? I have resisted answering that question, in part because I was still in the midst of my research and had not fully formulated my own conclusions. I can no longer use that reason. Yet I still resist answering the question, but for a different reason. This question of what someone *really* thinks about Jesse Jackson usually centers around evaluating him as a personality, not around his ideas or his political platform or agenda. It has been my goal in this book to demonstrate that— *whatever* one thinks about Jesse Jackson as a personality—his ideas deserve explication and examination. American politics, to its detriment, has too often devolved into personality contests rather than contests over issues. Unfortunately, because of the force of his personality, Jackson far too often plays right into this American tendency to personalize political issues. His rhetorical skill, for instance, can be so impressive that it is possible to miss the significance of what he is saying. His bold initiatives or his attempts to educate through controversy can make *him*, rather than *his ideas*, the issue.

But let me respond to the question that people *should* be asking— What about Jackson's candidacy and his vision for America? I believe that his candidacy is among the most hopeful and positive forces on the contemporary American scene. Four of the most important factors in this judgment are:

1. He asks broad questions about national purpose and priorities. While all presidential campaigns necessarily do this to some extent, few candidates address these questions as squarely as Jackson. Few have his skill at making complex issues understandable to ordinary citizens. He attempts to combine the "political" and the "prophetic" and correctly observes that, in the end, political issues are fundamentally questions about human values. Thus he asks questions such as: How are we to understand national greatness? What does it mean to be Number One? These questions call for reflection and perspective on the part of the electorate.

2. He challenges Americans first to understand their own needs and self-interests, then to seek common cause with others with similar needs, but finally to transcend these, to seek "moral higher ground," the common good. Like the questions about national priorities, these interrelated challenges grow out of his dual role as politician and prophet and are aimed at gaining perspective, at

reflective action rather than reflexive response. Implied in all of this is a deep commitment to democratic social change. As he observes, using the ballot box to bring about change keeps people from "exploding through riots" or "imploding through drugs."[1] This, Jackson correctly concludes, is "the genius of our democracy."[2]

3. He stresses interrelationships and interdependence, both between people and between problems. This is the basis for his attempting to build coalitions. His vision for America is an attempt to bring Americans together for larger purposes rather than driving them apart to seek their narrow self-interests. In recent decades, the world has become thoroughly interdependent. His emphasis on interdependence seems capable of providing some important guidance in foreign policy issues as well as domestic ones, assisting America in making "the psychological adjustment from being superior over to being equivalent with and sometimes dependent upon."[3]

4. He brings many new elements to American presidential politics. Three of these stand out:

New Groups. His candidacy has captured the imagination of many Americans who previously had not found any candidates who elicited their support or interest. He calls these America's "damned, disinherited, disrespected, and despised." In addition, I agree with Sheila Collins, who claims that Jackson has found ways to link "nonelectoral forms of political mobilization and protest with traditional electoral politics."[4] Much of this is due to his attempt to combine the prophetic and the political. As a result, he has broadened participation in electoral politics.

New Issues. At the very least, he has called attention to America's poor, to America's various people of color, and to all those who have not typically been part of ordinary political considerations. His candidacy itself—by raising the question of whether a black man can become president in America—has raised the issue of race to the political fore, a place it has not occupied for twenty years.

New Perspective. His perspective offers both criticism and hope. This is at the heart of his dual approach to America as both dream and reality and his dual role as prophet and politician. His perspective provides a powerful critique of things as they are, but it also provides principles for constructive change. Jackson is animated by a vision

133

for America which he articulates clearly and forcefully. This vision offers citizens new possibilities for both thought and action.

But there are limits to his approach and vision. For example, although his "perspective of the rejected" and his thorough and comprehensive understanding of racism explain far more of America's ills than most Americans would readily admit, racism does not explain everything wrong with America any more than such interpretive principles as "class" or "sex." While various problems in American society *are* linked, as he contends over and over as he attempts to establish his Rainbow Coalition of the rejected, solving one problem does not automatically solve others. He himself clearly recognizes this when it comes to racism in American life. He does not believe that dealing with class divisions or with sexism necessarily will eliminate racism. Yet this is not fully evident when he talks about leaving racial battlegrounds and coming to common economic ground.

Racism, however, remains America's great unsolved problem. W. E. B. DuBois does appear to have been right when he declared in 1903 that "the problem of the twentieth century is the color-line."[5] It is true that directly addressing racism and its effects could move the country in the direction of "humane priorities," thereby assisting Americans in addressing other problems. But addressing racism will not solve the problem of the growing gap between rich and poor in America, and it will not solve the problem of sexism. Thus because there are limits to the usefulness of Jackson's interpretive principle of racism (as there are with any principle), there also are limits to the kind of coalition politics he advocates.

But in discussing such limits, I am beginning to go beyond the bounds of this book. In the Introduction, I described several books recently written about Jackson and then addressed the particular angle of vision (and thus the limitations) of each. It seems appropriate to do this as well for *Beyond Opportunity*. I have focused on Jackson's ideas as contained in his speeches over the years and have attempted to explicate them. This kind of examination of Jackson necessarily is more sympathetic to him than a variety of other approaches would have been since it takes seriously his viewpoint and what he is saying. I have argued that understanding his ideas is essential to understanding him. But I have not argued that this is *all* one needs to understand. Certainly his personality is important, as are his political and administrative skills. Finally, the effectiveness of his efforts must be judged by a variety of standards: electoral achievements, changes in public understanding, faithfulness to the black church tradition, adherence to democratic principles, rhetorical skillfulness, or progress in addressing racism, to name but a few.

This book has not addressed any of these questions. One virtue of the approach I have taken in *Beyond Opportunity*, however, is that it allows readers to make their own informed judgments about Jackson's ideas and his vision for America. It is my hope that they will do this.

Notes

INTRODUCTION

1. "The Third Candidate's World," *New Republic,* July 30, 1984, p. 12.

2. Barry Commoner, "Jackson Candidacy Is Giving New Shape to Politics in U.S.," *New York Times,* April 13, 1984.

3. See, for example, Adolph L. Reed, Jr., *The Jesse Jackson Phenomenon: The Crisis of Purpose in Afro-American Politics* (New Haven: Yale University Press, 1986), 1.

4. Theodore White, "Jackson, Democratic Revolutionary," *New York Times,* April 5, 1984.

5. Barbara A. Reynolds, *Jesse Jackson: The Man, the Movement, the Myth* (Chicago: Nelson-Hall, 1975); reissued as *Jesse Jackson: America's David* (Washington, D.C.: JFJ Associates, 1985).

6. Thomas H. Landess and Richard M. Quinn, *Jesse Jackson and the Politics of Race* (Ottawa, Ill.: Jameson Books, 1985).

7. See n. 3 above.

8. Sheila D. Collins, *The Rainbow Challenge: The Jackson Campaign and the Future of U.S. Politics* (New York: Monthly Review Press, 1986).

9. Bob Faw and Nancy Skelton, *Thunder in America: The Improbable Presidential Campaign of Jesse Jackson* (Austin: Texas Monthly Press, 1986).

10. Landess and Quinn, *Jackson and Politics of Race,* 238.

11. Reed, *Jackson Phenomenon,* 1.

12. Ibid., 35.

13. Collins, *Rainbow Challenge,* 19.

14. James Melvin Washington, "Jesse Jackson and the Symbolic Politics of Black Christendom," *Annals of the American Academy of Political and Social Science* 480 (July 1985): 89–105.

15. Ibid., 96.

16. David S. Broder, "Have You Heard What Jackson Said?" syndicated

column, *Washington Post,* May 17, 1987. See also Morton Kondracke, "The Jacksonian Persuasion: He Too Has Ideas, and They Should Be Examined," *New Republic,* April 30, 1984, pp. 13–16.

17. "The Quest for a Just Society and a Peaceful World," Presidential Announcement Speech, Washington, D.C., November 3, 1983.

18. "The Vision of a New Course, a New Coalition, and a New Leadership," Twelfth Annual Operation PUSH Convention, Atlanta, July 27, 1983.

19. Jesse L. Jackson, *Straight from the Heart,* ed. Roger D. Hatch and Frank E. Watkins (Philadelphia: Fortress Press, 1987).

1. BEYOND OPPORTUNITY

1. Peter J. Paris, *The Social Teaching of the Black Churches* (Philadelphia: Fortress Press, 1985), 10.

2. See, for example, Vincent Harding, *There Is a River: The Black Struggle for Freedom in America* (New York: Random House, 1983). Harding argues that any way of denying the validity or truth of racism is a form of resistance. Accordingly, he includes actions often characterized as "romantic" or "escapist" and argues that suicide has been a form of resistance (see, for example, p. 20).

3. "Political Votes, Economic Oats," 26, and "We Must Act, Not Just React: The Present Challenge of Our Democracy," 38, in *Straight from the Heart,* by Jesse L. Jackson, ed. Roger D. Hatch and Frank E. Watkins (Philadelphia: Fortress Press, 1987).

4. Ibid.

5. See, for example, "Equity in a New World Order: Reparations and Reciprocity," in *Straight from the Heart,* 299.

6. Roger Wilkins, "The Natural," *Mother Jones* (August–September 1984): 40.

7. "The Quest for a Just Society and a Peaceful World," Presidential Announcement Speech, Washington, D.C., November 3, 1983: "The new covenant we seek with the Democratic Party is one that provides for full parity for blacks and the other elements of our Rainbow Coalition. . . . The new covenant we seek with the trade union movement is one that would provide for the swift elimination of all the remaining vestiges of racial discrimination in apprenticeship programs, seniority structures, and union staff and leadership opportunities. . . . The new covenant we seek with corporate America is one that would end the current restraint of trade practices that lock blacks, Hispanics, and other elements of the rainbow out of business opportunities and jobs."

8. Ibid. Here Jackson paraphrased Luke 4:18–19, which is an account of Jesus in the synagogue in Nazareth reading Isa. 61:1–2.

9. "The Candidate's Challenge: The Call of Conscience, the Courage of Conviction," in *Straight from the Heart,* 6. See also Matt. 9:17; Mark 2:22; Luke 5:37–38.

10. "From Battleground to Common Ground to Higher Ground," in *Straight from the Heart*, 143.

11. The biographical information that follows was drawn largely from chapter 2 of Barbara A. Reynolds, *Jesse Jackson: The Man, the Movement, the Myth* (Chicago: Nelson-Hall, 1975).

12. Preface, in *Straight from the Heart*, ix.

13. See Alan B. Anderson and George W. Pickering, *Confronting the Color Line: The Broken Promise of the Civil Rights Movement in Chicago* (Athens: University of Georgia Press, 1986), for a detailed account of CCCO's activities and their relation to the entire Civil Rights Movement.

14. For a history of the beginnings of Operation Breadbasket, see Gary Massoni, "Perspective on Operation Breadbasket" (M.Div. thesis, Chicago Theological Seminary, 1971).

15. Racism actually has been institutionalized in three major ways in America, not just one, as the term "institutional racism" implies: slavery, Jim Crow (legal segregation), and the metropolitan color line. The Civil War and Reconstruction addressed slavery; the Civil Rights Movement of the 1950s and 1960s addressed the Jim Crow institutional form of racism; and the metropolitan color line, racism's current institutionalized form, still remains to be addressed effectively. Jackson's activities have been aimed at eliminating the metropolitan color line rather than Jim Crow, and this accounts for many of the differences between Jackson's approach and the earlier Civil Rights Movement. (See Anderson and Pickering, *Confronting the Color Line*, esp. the introduction, 1–12. The term "metropolitan color line" is theirs.)

16. See "Overcoming New Forms of Denial," 106, and "Protecting the Legacy: The Challenge of Dr. Martin Luther King, Jr.," 127, in *Straight from the Heart*.

17. "Overcoming New Forms of Denial," 105–6, and "Protecting the Legacy," 127, in *Straight from the Heart*.

18. "The State of Black America and the Challenge to Overcome Against the Odds," Morehouse College, Atlanta, February 15, 1983.

19. "Dreaming New Dreams," in *Straight from the Heart*, 19–20.

20. See, for example, *"Brown* Twenty-five Years Later," in *Straight from the Heart*, 89.

21. "A Call to Action," Operation PUSH Saturday Morning Community Forum, Chicago, June 16, 1979.

22. *"Brown* Twenty-four Years Later: Where Do We Go from Here?" Operation PUSH Saturday Morning Community Forum, Chicago, June 3, 1978. See also *"Brown* Twenty-five Years Later," in *Straight from the Heart*, 89.

23. *"Brown* Twenty-five Years Later," in *Straight from the Heart*, 89.

24. "From Battleground to Common Ground to Higher Ground," in *Straight from the Heart*, 141.

25. "Affirmative Action: Clarifying Some of the Issues," Universal Press Syndicate, December 6, 1981.

26. "Dreaming New Dreams," in *Straight from the Heart*, 20.

27. Martin Luther King, Jr., *Where Do We Go from Here: Chaos or Community?* (New York: Harper & Row, 1967), 157.

28. Ibid., 4.

29. Ibid., 6.

30. Ibid., 5.

31. Ibid., 168–72.

32. Ibid., 173–83 passim.

33. Ibid., 4.

34. *"Brown* Twenty-five Years Later," 89, "Save Our Children: Administrators for Excellence," 201, and "Excellence in the Press: Freedom, Fairness, and the Future," 324, in *Straight from the Heart.*

35. Youth Rally, Sixth Annual Operation PUSH Convention, Los Angeles, July 1977.

36. Booker T. Washington, "The Atlanta Exposition Address, September 1895," in *Up from Slavery* (New York: Doubleday, Page & Co., 1909), 218–25, as reprinted in August Meier, Elliott Rudwick, and Francis L. Broderick, eds., *Black Protest Thought in the Twentieth Century* (Indianapolis: Bobbs-Merrill, 1971), 5.

37. "The Quest for Jobs, Peace, and Justice," NAACP Annual Convention, New York, July 8, 1987.

38. Jackson, however, attempts to show many white people that they too are victimized by racism and, thus, that it also is in their self-interest to create racial justice.

39. "The State of Black America and the Challenge to Overcome Against the Odds," February 15, 1983.

40. "Where There Is No Vision, the People Perish," Operation PUSH Saturday Morning Community Forum, Chicago, January 24, 1981.

2. TOWARD A NEW AMERICA

1. "Meet the Press," NBC-TV, April 8, 1984.

2. In this chapter, I am using the terms "America" and "United States" synonymously. Although America as a geographical designation properly refers to all of the countries of the Western hemisphere and not just to the United States, America as an idea most often refers only to that part of the Americas that became the United States. Since the idea of America is not equivalent with the idea of the United States, I have chosen to use the term America.

3. "Affirmative Action: Tool for Social Justice," Universal Press Syndicate, November 29, 1981.

4. "Overcoming New Forms of Denial," in *Straight from the Heart*, by

Jesse L. Jackson, ed. Roger D. Hatch and Frank E. Watkins (Philadelphia: Fortress Press, 1987), 105.

5. "We Must Act, Not Just React: The Present Challenge of Our Democracy," in *Straight from the Heart*, 38–39.

6. "Overcoming New Forms of Denial," in *Straight from the Heart*, 105.

7. "The Candidate's Challenge: The Call of Conscience, the Courage of Conviction," in *Straight from the Heart*, 5.

8. William B. Gravely, "The'Dialectic of Double-Consciousness in Black American Freedom Celebrations, 1808–1863," *Journal of Negro History* 67, no. 4 (Winter 1982): 302–17, esp. 311.

9. Thurgood Marshall, speech at the annual seminar of the San Francisco Patent and Trademark Law Association, meeting in Maui, Hawaii, May 6, 1987, as quoted in the *New York Times*, May 7, 1987. The complete text appears in *Ebony*, September 1987, pp. 62–68.

10. Ibid.

11. Langston Hughes, "Let America Be America Again," *A New Song* (New York: International Workers Order, 1938). See Jackson's use in "A Call to Community," B'nai Brith, Framingham, Mass., March 4, 1984.

12. Gunnar Myrdal, *An American Dilemma: The Negro Problem and Modern Democracy*, 2 vols. (New York: Harper & Brothers, 1944), 1:4.

13. "The Importance of the Black College," Universal Press Syndicate, February 25, 1979.

14. "From Battleground to Common Ground to Higher Ground," in *Straight from the Heart*, 142.

15. "Forty Years Later—Liberation, But Not Yet Joy," in *Straight from the Heart*, 255.

16. For example, in the early 1940s, Swedish social scientist Gunnar Myrdal used this framework in his classic analysis of "the Negro problem," *An American Dilemma.*

17. Ronald Reagan, as quoted in the *New York Times*, July 4, 1986.

18. It is important to note not only that Reagan's dream of America lies in the past and Jackson's in the future but that the substance of their dreams for America is different.

19. "The Quest for a Just Society and a Peaceful World," Presidential Announcement Speech, Washington, D.C., November 3, 1983.

20. Ibid.

21. "We Must Act, Not Just React," 40, and "Save Our Children: Administrators for Excellence," 197, in *Straight from the Heart.*

22. "Affirmative Action: Tool for Social Justice," November 29, 1981.

23. William Julius Wilson, *The Declining Significance of Race* (Chicago: University of Chicago Press, 1978).

24. "The State of Black America and the Challenge to Overcome Against the Odds," Morehouse College, Atlanta, February 15, 1983.

25. Roger Simon, "Voters Still Not Color Blind," Los Angeles Times Syndicate, July 10, 1987.

26. "Service and a New World Order," in *Straight from the Heart,* 79.

27. Ibid.

28. "PUSH for Excellence Can Be One of the Cures," *Ebony,* September 1979. See also "In Pursuit of Peace—A More Excellent Way," in *Straight from the Heart,* 222.

29. "The Tragedy and the Treasure of South Africa," Operation PUSH Saturday Morning Community Forum, Chicago, August 3, 1979.

30. "We Must Act, Not Just React," 45, "Overcoming New Forms of Denial," 104, and "Save Our Children," 195, in *Straight from the Heart.*

31. "Service and a New World Order," in *Straight from the Heart,* 79.

32. Ibid.

33. "Overcoming New Forms of Denial," in *Straight from the Heart,* 104.

34. "The State of the Nation: An Alternative View," Northeastern University, Boston, January 31, 1984. See also "We Must Act, Not Just React," in *Straight from the Heart,* 38.

35. "In Pursuit of Equity, Ethics and Excellence: The Challenge to Close the Gap," Department of Health, Education, and Welfare, Washington, D.C., January 25, 1979.

36. "Service and a New World Order," in *Straight from the Heart,* 79.

37. "The Challenge to Live in One World," Operation PUSH Saturday Morning Community Forum, Chicago, October 13, 1979.

38. "From Battleground to Common Ground to Higher Ground," in *Straight from the Heart,* 139.

39. "The Candidate's Challenge," 18 (see also 16), and "Forty Years Later—Liberation, But Not Yet Joy," 253, in *Straight from the Heart.*

40. Address to Demonstration Against Intervention in Central America and the Caribbean, Washington, D.C., November 12, 1983.

41. Ibid.

42. Ibid.

43. "The State of Black America and the Challenge to Overcome Against the Odds," February 15, 1983.

44. See, for example, Address at Dartmouth University, Hanover, N.H., January 19, 1984. Martin Luther King, Jr., argued much the same position in *Where Do We Go from Here: Chaos or Community?* (New York: Harper & Row, 1967), writing of "two dominant and contradictory strains in the American psyche, the positive one, our democratic heritage, . . . and [the negative one], racism" (p. 83).

45. "An End to Corporate Blackmail," in *Straight from the Heart,* 312–13.

46. "The Candidate's Challenge," 12, "We Must Act, Not Just React," 41, 46, "Save Our Children," 196, and "It's Up to You," 212, in *Straight from the Heart.*

47. "A Challenge to the New Generation," *Ebony,* August 1978, p. 164.

48. "Peace Through Justice: The Crisis in Central America," in *Straight from the Heart,* 247.

49. Ibid.

50. "Overcoming New Forms of Denial," in *Straight from the Heart,* 104.

51. "The Quest for a Just Society and a Peaceful World," November 3, 1983.

52. "A Better Way for America," Keene Junior High School, Keene, N.H., February 16, 1984. See also "The Candidate's Challenge," 12, and "An End to Corporate Blackmail," 312, in *Straight from the Heart.*

53. "The State of the Nation: An Alternative View," January 31, 1984.

54. "Keys to a Democratic Victory in 1984, "Thirteenth Annual Operation PUSH Convention, Charleston, S.C., June 7, 1984.

55. "Peace and the Crisis in Central America," Cathedral of St. John the Divine, New York, March 29, 1984.

56. "An End to Corporate Blackmail," in *Straight from the Heart,* 314.

57. Preface, in *Straight from the Heart,* ix.

58. See n. 11.

59. Isa. 61:1–2a, RSV. See also Luke 4:16–21 and "The Candidate's Challenge," in *Straight from the Heart,* 3.

60. Matt. 25:40b, KJV.

61. "The Quest for a Just Society and a Peaceful World," November 3, 1983. See also "The Candidate's Challenge," 7, 18, "Protecting the Legacy: The Challenge of Dr. Martin Luther King, Jr.," 131, and "Save the Family Farm and the Farm Family," 283, in *Straight from the Heart.*

62. "Service and a New World Order," 82, and "From Battleground to Common Ground to Higher Ground," 138, in *Straight from the Heart.*

63. "Service and a New World Order," 82, "Protecting the Legacy," 126, "In Pursuit of Peace—A More Excellent Way," 221, "Forty Years Later— Liberation, But Not Yet Joy," 256, and "Excellence in the Press: Freedom, Fairness, and the Future," 324, in *Straight from the Heart.*

64. Speech to World Affairs Council, Vancouver, Washington, April 4, 1984.

65. Speech in Panama City, Panama, June 23, 1984.

66. "An End to Corporate Blackmail," in *Straight from the Heart,* 314.

67. Address at Dartmouth University, Hanover, N.H., January 19, 1984. Note, however, that Jackson does not believe that justice or the right will automatically prevail because of the forces of history; it takes disciplined, organized, and persistent action by human beings to achieve justice.

68. The phrase is Thomas Jefferson's, first used in a January 1, 1802, letter to the Danbury, Connecticut, Baptist Association.

69. Robert Bellah, "Civil Religion in America," in *American Civil Religion,* ed. Russell E. Richey and Donald G. Jones (New York: Harper & Row, 1974), 42 n. 3.

70. Herbert Richardson, "Civil Religion in Theological Perspective," in *American Civil Religion,* ed. Richey and Jones, 170–71.

71. Bellah, "Civil Religion in America," 25.

72. "The Keys to a Democratic Victory in 1984," Position Paper, 1984.

73. Preface, in *Straight from the Heart,* ix.

74. See n. 9.

75. Farmworker and Community Rally, Vineland, N.J., May 25, 1984.

76. Address at Dartmouth University, Hanover, N.H., January 19, 1984.

77. "A Call to Community," March 4, 1984.

78. "Foreign Policy—But Not Foreign Values," in *Straight from the Heart,* 227.

79. "Keys to a Democratic Victory in 1984," June 7, 1984.

80. "Arab-Americans and the Rainbow Coalition," American-Arab Anti-Discrimination Convention, Los Angeles, November 5, 1983.

81. "The State of the Nation: An Alternative View," January 31, 1984.

82. "The Unfinished Business of the Democratic Convention," Operation PUSH Saturday Morning Community Forum, Chicago, July 28, 1984.

83. "Environmental Justice: A Call to Action," in *Straight from the Heart,* 307.

84. Preface, in *Straight from the Heart,* ix.

3. HUMANE PRIORITIES AT HOME

1. "Arab-Americans and the Rainbow Coalition," American-Arab Anti-Discrimination Convention, Los Angeles, November 5, 1983.

2. "The Candidate's Challenge: The Call of Conscience, the Courage of Conviction," in *Straight from the Heart,* by Jesse L. Jackson, ed. Roger D. Hatch and Frank E. Watkins (Philadelphia: Fortress Press, 1987), 17.

3. "Save Our Children: Administrators for Excellence," in *Straight from the Heart,* 198.

4. Ibid., 197.

5. See accounts by Carl T. Rowan, "Coca-Cola Makes Boardrooms Fizz," *Chicago Sun-Times,* December 30, 1981; Monroe Anderson, "Boycott Victory Puts Life in PUSH," *Chicago Tribune,* December 20, 1981; and Johnnie L. Roberts, "Threatening Boycotts, Jesse Jackson's PUSH Makes Gains for Blacks," *Wall Street Journal,* July 21, 1982.

6. Rowan, "Coca-Cola Makes Boardrooms Fizz."

7. See, for example, the positive, front-page story in the *Wall Street Journal* (n. 5 above) on PUSH's signing a covenant with Coca-Cola.

8. "Affirmative Action: Tool for Social Justice," Universal Press Syndicate, November 29, 1981.

9. "Black Americans and the Private Sector," Universal Press Syndicate, December 21, 1980.

10. "Equity in a New World Order: Reparations and Reciprocity," 301, and "Black Americans Seek Equity and Parity," 279, in *Straight from the Heart.*

11. "Development Formula Needed for Black America," Universal Press Syndicate, July 26, 1981.

12. "Black Americans and the Private Sector," December 21, 1980.

13. "Equity in a New World Order," in *Straight from the Heart,* 300.

14. "Development Formula Needed for Black America," July 26, 1981.

15. "Black Challenge of the 1980s: Not Aid But Trade," Universal Press Syndicate, January 10, 1982.

16. Ibid. See also "Black Americans Seek Economic Equity and Parity," in *Straight from the Heart,* 279.

17. "Black Americans Seek Economic Equity and Parity," in *Straight from the Heart,* 279.

18. "Development Formula Needed for Black America," July 26, 1981.

19. See, for example, Keynote Speech for the National United Affiliated Beverage Association National Convention Awards Banquet, Chicago, September 29, 1982.

20. "The Unfinished Business of the Democratic Convention," Operation PUSH Saturday Morning Community Forum, Chicago, July 28, 1984.

21. "Black Americans Seek Economic Equity and Parity," in *Straight from the Heart,* 278–79.

22. "The Rejected Stones: The Cornerstones of a New Public Policy," National Press Club, Washington, D.C., May 10, 1983.

23. See, for example, "From Battleground to Common Ground to Higher Ground," in *Straight from the Heart,* 137–45.

24. "The State of the Nation: An Alternative View," Northeastern University, Boston, January 31, 1984.

25. "The Rejected Stones," May 10, 1983.

26. A typical speech is "Save Our Children," in *Straight from the Heart,* 194–204.

27. A typical speech is "It's Up to You," in *Straight from the Heart,* 205–12.

28. Named after Alan Bakke (and the 1978 Supreme Court decision bearing his name), a white male who claimed he was the victim of "reverse discrimination" in his attempt to be admitted to medical school at the University of California–Davis. The Supreme Court's decision ambiguously affirmed both the principle of affirmative action for victims of historic discrimination and Bakke's claim that he had been unfairly discriminated against.

29. "It's Up to You," in *Straight from the Heart,* 201.

30. Ibid.

31. Ibid., 199.

32. Ibid.

33. Ibid., 212.

34. Ibid., 210.

35. Ibid., 207.

36. "Save Our Children," in *Straight from the Heart,* 201.

37. "It's Up to You," in *Straight from the Heart,* 212.

38. "Save Our Children," in *Straight from the Heart,* 204.

39. "The Ten Commandments for Excellence in Education," in *Straight from the Heart,* 184–86.

40. David S. Broder, "Have You Heard What Jackson Said?" syndicated column, *Washington Post,* May 17, 1987.

41. "Eliminate Hunger: A Birthday Present Fit for Dr. Martin Luther King, Jr.," Harvard University, Cambridge, Mass., January 15, 1985.

42. "What Does the Government Owe the Poor?" in *Straight from the Heart,* 266.

43. "Save the Family Farm and the Farm Family," in *Straight from the Heart,* 286–87.

44. "The Candidate's Challenge," in *Straight from the Heart,* 8.

45. "Poverty in the Midst of Plenty," Knoxville, Tenn., April 22, 1984.

46. "Eliminate Hunger," January 15, 1985.

47. "Save the Family Farm and the Farm Family," in *Straight from the Heart,* 287.

48. "Bombs or Bread," Universal Press Syndicate, January 17, 1982. Jackson is drawing on "The Empty Porkbarrel," a study of the effects of military spending on the economy conducted by Marion Anderson of Employment Research Associates, Lansing, Mich.

49. "Eliminate Hunger," January 15, 1985.

50. "The Keys to a Democratic Victory in 1984," Thirteenth Annual Operation PUSH Convention, Charleston, S.C., June 7, 1984.

51. "The Candidate's Challenge," in *Straight from the Heart,* 15.

52. See, for example, "Save the Family Farm and the Farm Family," in *Straight from the Heart,* 282–88.

53. Ibid., 282.

54. Ibid., 287.

55. Ibid., 286–88.

56. Barry Commoner, "The Case for Jackson," *Village Voice,* April 3, 1984.

57. "Protecting the Legacy: The Challenge of Dr. Martin Luther King, Jr.," in *Straight from the Heart,* 131.

4. HUMAN RIGHTS FOR ALL HUMAN BEINGS

1. "The Third Candidate's World," *New Republic,* July 30, 1984, p. 12.

2. See, for example, his condemnation of U.S. foreign policy in Southern Africa, Central America, and Chile, "A Call to Community," B'nai Brith, Framingham, Mass., March 4, 1984. See also "An End to Corporate Blackmail," in *Straight from the Heart,* by Jesse L. Jackson, ed. Roger D. Hatch and Frank E. Watkins (Philadelphia: Fortress Press, 1987), 314.

3. "The Rejected Stones: The Cornerstones of a New Public Policy," National Press Club, Washington, D.C., May 10, 1983. See also "Measuring Human Rights by One Yardstick," in *Straight from the Heart,* 73–75.

4. "Service and a New World Order," in *Straight from the Heart,* 83.

5. "Peace Through Justice: The Crisis in Central America," in *Straight from the Heart,* 248.

6. "Service and a New World Order," in *Straight from the Heart,* 79.

7. "The State of the Nation: An Alternative View," Northeastern University, Boston, January 31, 1984.

8. "The Candidate's Challenge: The Call of Conscience, the Courage of Conviction," 14; see also "Dreaming New Dreams," 21, "Measuring Human Rights by One Yardstick," 75, and "Foreign Policy—But Not Foreign Values," 228, in *Straight from the Heart*.

9. Address to Demonstration Against Intervention in Central America and the Caribbean, Washington, D.C., November 12, 1983. See also "The Candidate's Challenge," in *Straight from the Heart*, 6.

10. See, for example, "A Call to Community," March 4, 1984.

11. "Meet the Press," NBC-TV, April 8, 1984.

12. "A Quest for Peace in the Middle East—And the Vital Interests of Black People," Operation PUSH Saturday Morning Community Forum, Chicago, August 20, 1979. See also "Service and a New World Order," 82, "Protecting the Legacy: The Challenge of Dr. Martin Luther King, Jr.," 126, 130, "In Pursuit of Peace—A More Excellent Way," 221, "Forty Years Later—Liberation, But Not Yet Joy," 256, and "Excellence in the Press: Freedom, Fairness, and the Future," 324, in *Straight from the Heart*.

13. "A Call to Community," March 4, 1984.

14. "Protecting the Legacy," in *Straight from the Heart*, 126.

15. "Peace Through Justice," in *Straight from the Heart*, 248.

16. "The State of the Nation: An Alternative View," January 31, 1984.

17. "The Keys to a Democratic Victory in 1984," Thirteenth Annual Operation PUSH Convention, Charleston, S.C., June 7, 1984. See also "Peace Through Justice," in *Straight from the Heart*, 249.

18. "The Keys to a Democratic Victory in 1984," June 7, 1984. See also "Peace Through Justice," in *Straight from the Heart*, 247.

19. Press statement on demonstrations in South Korea, June 15, 1987.

20. "Foreign Policy—But Not Foreign Values," in *Straight from the Heart*, 226.

21. Prov. 29:18a, KJV.

22. Speech in Panama City, Panama, June 23, 1984. What needs to be recognized is that "the people's will cannot be stopped. No amount of military means of destruction can be ultimately successful."

23. "A Call to Community," March 4, 1984; and "A Call to Trialogue," Arab-American Anti-Discrimination Committee Convention, Washington, D.C., March 18, 1984.

24. Speech to World Affairs Council, Vancouver, Washington, April 4, 1984. See also "Service and a New World Order," 84, and "Foreign Policy—But Not Foreign Values," 224, in *Straight from the Heart*.

25. "Service and a New World Order," in *Straight from the Heart*, 84.

26. Ibid.

27. "Arab-Americans and the Rainbow Coalition," American-Arab Anti-Discrimination Convention, Los Angeles, November 5, 1983. See also "In Search of a New Focus and a New Vision," in *Straight from the Heart*, 101.

28. "In Search of a New Focus and a New Vision," in *Straight from the Heart*, 101.

29. "Foreign Policy—But Not Foreign Values," in *Straight from the Heart*, 228.

30. "In Search of a New Focus and a New Vision," 97, "Protecting the Legacy," 128, "From Battleground to Common Ground to Higher Ground," 139–40, and "An End to Corporate Blackmail," 313, in *Straight from the Heart*.

31. See, for example, "The Candidate's Challenge," in *Straight from the Heart*, 8–11.

32. "A Policy for Peace," Franklin Pierce College, Rindge, N.H., February 15, 1984.

33. Speech in Panama City, Panama, June 23, 1984.

34. See, for example, "The Vision of a New Course, a New Coalition, and a New Leadership," Twelfth Annual Operation PUSH Convention, Atlanta, July 27, 1983: "Our national security is being threatened from within because of a shaky and unjust distribution of our economic wealth."

35. "The State of the Nation: An Alternative View," January 31, 1984.

36. *Playboy*, June 1984, p. 76.

37. "Service and a New World Order," in *Straight from the Heart*, 84.

38. Speech to World Affairs Council, Vancouver, Washington, April 4, 1984.

39. See, for example, "Religious Liberty: Civil Disobedience, Conscience, and Survival," in *Straight from the Heart*, 147.

40. See "Foreign Policy—But Not Foreign Values," in *Straight from the Heart*, 226.

41. See "A Quest for Peace in the Middle East—And the Vital Interests of Black People," August 20, 1979. See also "Foreign Policy—But Not Foreign Values," in *Straight from the Heart*, 226.

42. "The Middle East," Jackson Campaign Position Paper, 1984.

43. Ibid.

44. Ibid.

45. See "The Tragedy and the Treasure of South Africa," Operation PUSH Saturday Morning Community Forum, Chicago, August 3, 1979.

46. "American Options on Apartheid," in *Straight from the Heart*, 239.

47. "The Tragedy and the Treasure of South Africa," August 3, 1979.

48. "American Options on Apartheid," in *Straight from the Heart*, 245.

49. Speech at League of United Latin American Citizens Convention, San Antonio, May 3, 1984.

50. See, for example, Jackson's six-point stance in "Peace Through Justice," in *Straight from the Heart*, 248–49.

51. "Meet the Press," April 8, 1984.

52. See, for example, Martin Luther King, Jr., *Where Do We Go from Here: Chaos or Community?* (New York: Harper & Row, 1967), chap. 6, "The World House," esp. 211–16.

53. Media and Presidential Campaigns Issues Forum, University of Missouri–Columbia Journalism School, April 16, 1984.

54. "The Challenge to Live in One World," Operation PUSH Saturday Morning Community Forum, Chicago, October 13, 1979.

55. "Service and a New World Order," in *Straight from the Heart*, 83.

56. Media and Presidential Campaigns Issues Forum, University of Missouri–Columbia Journalism School, April 16, 1984.

5. PROGRESSIVE SOCIAL CHANGE

1. "Religious Liberty: Civil Disobedience, Conscience, and Survival," 150, and "It's Up to You," 207–8, 212, in *Straight from the Heart*, by Jesse L. Jackson, ed. Roger D. Hatch and Frank E. Watkins (Philadelphia: Fortress Press, 1987).

2. "Politics as an Educational Forum," Ford Hall Forum, Boston, March 27, 1983.

3. "The Rejected Stones: The Cornerstones of a New Public Policy," National Press Club, Washington, D.C., May 10, 1983.

4. "Short-Term Pleasure and Long-Term Pain: The Challenge and Responsibility of Making Decisions," PUSH for Excellence Reproductive Health and Health Careers Conference, Chicago, November 14, 1978.

5. "Service and a New World Order," in *Straight from the Heart*, 78.

6. Ibid.

7. "The Candidate's Challenge: The Call of Conscience, the Courage of Conviction," in *Straight from the Heart*, 5.

8. "An End to Corporate Blackmail," in *Straight from the Heart*, 312–13.

9. "The Candidate's Challenge," in *Straight from the Heart*, 5.

10. "Service and a New World Order," in *Straight from the Heart*, 78.

11. "Set a New Agenda: Justice at Home, Peace Abroad," *New York Times*, February 27, 1984.

12. "The Candidate's Challenge," in *Straight from the Heart*, 16.

13. "Liberation and Justice: A Call for Redefinition, Refocus, and Rededication," in *Straight from the Heart*, 63.

14. "The Candidate's Challenge," 18, "Service and a New World Order," 85, "Binding Up the Wounds," 135, and "Forty Years Later—Liberation, But Not Yet Joy," 257, in *Straight from the Heart*.

15. "The Candidate's Challenge," in *Straight from the Heart*, 17. Jackson made a similar point in speeches before joint sessions of the Louisiana and South Carolina legislatures: "I want to suggest another definition of our fundamental problem. The dominant characteristic and common ailment in our society today is a sense of hopelessness. Too many of us have lost hope. We have given up. We have dropped out. We think our economic problems are beyond our ability to cope with them. . . . We think our racial divisions are too deep. . . . We cannot communicate with our young people. . . . The fundamental issue confronting America today is not so much that Americans

need *help*—jobs, curbing inflation, balancing the budget, etc. No, the issue is the restoration of hope. . . . If leaders provide hope, people can help themselves. If leaders can keep hope alive, people will keep hopping. . . . We must not let . . . external problems and circumstances break our internal spirit. . . . We must revive the spirit of hope and optimism in our people" (December 13, 1983, and January 24, 1984).

16. "The Ten Commandments for Excellence in Education," in *Straight from the Heart,* 187.

17. "Dreaming New Dreams," in *Straight from the Heart,* 19.

18. "From Battleground to Common Ground to Higher Ground," in *Straight from the Heart,* 143.

19. "From Battleground to Common Ground to Higher Ground," 137–45, "The Candidate's Challenge," 16, and "Forty Years Later—Liberation, But Not Yet Joy," 253, in *Straight from the Heart.*

20. "Foreign Policy—But Not Foreign Values," in *Straight from the Heart,* 226.

21. "The Candidate's Challenge," in *Straight from the Heart,* 17–18.

22. "The Quest for a Just Society and a Peaceful World," Presidential Announcement Speech, Washington, D.C., November 3, 1983.

23. "Why I Want to Be President of the United States," Position Paper, 1984. Note that this quotation contains all three of Jackson's basic ideas: (1) We must respect ourselves and others. (2) Nutrition, education, housing, health care, and meaningful employment are all interrelated. (3) Greatness lies in acting on the basis of a vision beyond self-interest.

24. "The Ten Commandments for Excellence in Education," in *Straight from the Heart,* 186.

25. Ibid., 185.

26. See, for example, "Religious Liberty," in *Straight from the Heart,* 152–53.

27. "The Candidate's Challenge," 18, "In Search of a New Focus and a New Vision," 102, "Binding Up the Wounds," 135, and "Religious Liberty," 147, in *Straight from the Heart.*

28. "The Candidate's Challenge," 18, "Service and a New World Order," 85, "Binding Up the Wounds," 135, and "Forty Years Later—Liberation, But Not Yet Joy," 257, in *Straight from the Heart.*

29. "The Candidate's Challenge," in *Straight from the Heart,* 18.

30. See, for example, "The Candidate's Challenge," 18, "Religious Liberty," 147, and "The Ten Commandments for Excellence in Education," 186, in *Straight from the Heart.*

31. "*Brown* Twenty-five Years Later," 89, "Save Our Children: Administrators for Excellence," 201, and "Excellence in the Press: Freedom, Fairness, and the Future," 324, in *Straight from the Heart.*

32. "In Pursuit of Equity, Ethics and Excellence: The Challenge to Close the Gap," Morehouse College, Atlanta, February 15, 1979.

33. "A Better Way for America," Keene Junior High School, Keene, N.H., February 16, 1984.

34. "In Search of a New Focus and a New Vision," in *Straight from the Heart*, 101.

35. "The State of the Nation: An Alternative View," Northeastern University, Boston, January 31, 1984.

36. "Save Our Children," in *Straight from the Heart*, 201.

37. "In Pursuit of Peace—A More Excellent Way," in *Straight from the Heart*, 221.

38. "A Challenge to the New Generation," *Ebony*, August 1978, p. 164. See also "Service and a New World Order," 83, and "From Battleground to Common Ground to Higher Ground," 140, in *Straight from the Heart*.

39. "A Call to Action," Operation PUSH Saturday Morning Community Forum, Chicago, June 16, 1979.

40. "Save Our Children," in *Straight from the Heart*, 199.

41. "Political Votes, Economic Oats," in *Straight from the Heart*, 35.

42. "A Call to Action," June 16, 1979.

43. "Victim-Victimizer: Why Excel?" in *Straight from the Heart*, 190.

44. Ibid., 189.

45. "The Candidate's Challenge," in *Straight from the Heart*, 18.

46. "From Battleground to Common Ground to Higher Ground," 139, "We Must Act, Not Just React: The Present Challenge of Our Democracy," 46, "Save Our Children," 201, and "It's Up to You," 212, in *Straight from the Heart*.

47. "In Pursuit of Equity, Ethics and Excellence," February 15, 1979.

48. Ibid.

49. "Service and a New World Order," in *Straight from the Heart*, 85.

50. "Challenge to the New Generation," *Ebony*, August 1978, p. 164.

51. "Service and a New World Order," in *Straight from the Heart*, 77, 78.

52. "Religious Liberty," in *Straight from the Heart*, 151.

53. "A Call to Action," June 16, 1979.

54. "In Pursuit of Equity, Ethics and Excellence," February 15, 1979.

55. "Victim-Victimizer," in *Straight from the Heart*, 189.

56. "The Rejected Stones," May 10, 1983.

57. Gunnar Myrdal, "Appendix 3: A Methodological Note on the Principle of Cumulation," in *An American Dilemma: The Negro Problem and Modern Democracy*, 2 vols. (New York: Harper & Brothers, 1944), 2:1067.

58. See also ibid., 1069.

59. Operation PUSH Saturday Morning Community Forum, Chicago, August 26, 1978.

60. "The Candidate's Challenge," in *Straight from the Heart*, 5.

61. "From Battleground to Common Ground to Higher Ground," 143, and "Service and a New World Order," 83, in *Straight from the Heart*.

62. "Dreaming New Dreams," in *Straight from the Heart*, 21.

63. "A Quest for Peace in the Middle East—And the Vital Interests of Black People," Position Paper, August 20, 1979. See also "Service and a New World Order," 84, "Protecting the Legacy: The Challenge of Dr. Martin Luther King, Jr.," 126–27, and "Excellence in the Press," 319, in *Straight from the Heart.*

64. "The Rejected Stones," May 10, 1983.

65. "The State of Black America and the Challenge to Overcome Against the Odds," Morehouse College, Atlanta, February 15, 1983.

66. "Political Votes, Economic Oats," in *Straight from the Heart*, 25.

67. "We Must Act, Not Just React," in *Straight from the Heart*, 38.

68. "The Candidate's Challenge," in *Straight from the Heart*, 14.

69. "Service and a New World Order," 78, and "From Battleground to Common Ground to Higher Ground," 138, in *Straight from the Heart.*

70. "Religious Liberty," in *Straight from the Heart*, 147.

71. "Service and a New World Order," in *Straight from the Heart*, 78.

72. "Foreign Policy—But Not Foreign Values," in *Straight from the Heart*, 229.

73. "A Better Way for America," February 16, 1984.

74. "The Candidate's Challenge," in *Straight from the Heart*, 16.

75. See, for example, William B. Gravely, "The Dialectic of Double-Consciousness in Black American Freedom Celebrations, 1808–1863," *Journal of Negro History*, 67, no. 4 (Winter 1982): 302–17.

76. W. E. B. DuBois, *The Souls of Black Folk* (Greenwich, Conn.: Fawcett Books, 1961; originally published in 1903), 17.

77. I describe these three approaches to seeking racial justice at more length in "Racism and Religion: The Contrasting Views of Benjamin Mays, Malcolm X, and Martin Luther King, Jr.," *Journal of Religious Thought* 36, no. 2 (Fall–Winter 1979–80): 26–36. I argue there that black Americans have approached American culture in three classic ways: (1) a basic acceptance of the ideals of white American culture and an attempt to bring black reality into line with them (assimilation); (2) a basic rejection of white American cultural ideals and an attempt to substitute a new set of values (separation); and (3) a call for the transformation of American culture by carefully pursuing the best of both black and white values (transformation). Much of the confusion surrounding the term "integration" in the mid- and late 1960s was due to the fact that some (usually white) were using it to mean "assimilation" while others (usually black) were using it to mean "transformation." I contend that W. E. B. DuBois and Martin Luther King, Jr., were advocates of the transformationist position. Jesse Jackson clearly is. In addition to the pluralistic and transformationist imagery he employs to distinguish himself from assimilationists, he makes clear his disagreements with white liberals, whom he associates with the assimilation approach: "White liberals are willing to showcase blacks but not to share power. White liberals' agenda for blacks is participation, but the black agenda is liberation.

151

White liberals' agenda is freedom, but the black agenda is equality" ("The State of Black America and the Challenge to Overcome Against the Odds," February 15, 1983).

78. "Where There is No Vision, the People Perish," Operation PUSH Saturday Morning Community Forum, Chicago, January 24, 1981.

79. "Service and a New World Order," in *Straight from the Heart*, 82.

80. "The State of Black America and the Challenge to Overcome Against the Odds," February 15, 1983. See also "Black Americans Seek Economic Equity and Parity," in *Straight from the Heart*, 279.

81. "What Does the Government Owe the Poor?" in *Straight from the Heart*, 262.

82. "The Quest for Parity and Self-Respect," American Society of Newspaper Publishers and Editors, May 9, 1984.

83. "The Quest for a Just Society and a Peaceful World," November 3, 1983.

84. "The Third Candidate's World," *New Republic*, July 30, 1984, p. 12.

85. See "Black Americans Seek Economic Equity and Parity," in *Straight from the Heart*, esp. 280–81.

86. "Protecting the Legacy," in *Straight from the Heart*, 124.

87. "The Unfinished Business of the Democratic Convention," Operation PUSH Saturday Morning Community Forum, Chicago, July 28, 1984.

88. Julius Lester, "You Can't Go Home Again: Critical Thoughts About Jesse Jackson," *Dissent* (Winter 1985): 21.

89. William Safire, "Why Jackson Won't Disavow His Separatist Supporter," *New York Times*, April 10, 1984.

90. See chapter 2 for a more full discussion of this point.

91. Arthur Cohen long ago put the matter succinctly: "The fundamental problem of religion in a free society arises from the fact that religion tends to assert absolute claims and judgments, whereas the free society tends to insist that freedom can only thrive where all claims are treated as if they were relative" ("The Problem of Pluralism," in *Religion and the Free Society*, ed. William Lee Miller et al. [New York: Fund for the Republic, 1960]). In *The Jesse Jackson Phenomenon: The Crisis of Purpose in Afro-American Politics* (New Haven: Yale University Press, 1986) Adolph L. Reed, Jr., offers a related kind of criticism of the black church in general and of Jackson's 1984 campaign in particular. He argues that "an essential incompatibility, if not antagonism" (p. 60), exists between the church and politics. This is due to "the church's intrinsically antitemporal eschatological orientation" (p. 57) and its "model of authority that is antithetical to participatory representation" (p. 56).

92. Reinhold Niebuhr argued much the same way in "The Ethical Attitudes of the Proletarian Class" in *Moral Man and Immoral Society* (New York: Charles Scribner's Sons, 1960; originally published in 1932): "[The proletarian] does not differ from the privileged classes in attempting this uni-

versalisation of his particular values. . . . [Yet] the fact that the equalitarian ideal does not spring from pure ethical imagination, but is the result of the peculiar circumstances of proletarian life, does not detract from its validity as the ultimate social ideal" (pp. 153, 160).

93. "Political Votes, Economic Oats," in *Straight from the Heart*, 33.

94. Ibid.

95. "Environmental Justice: A Call to Action," in *Straight from the Heart*, 307.

6. JESSE JACKSON AND CONTROVERSY

1. See David A. Coolidge, Jr., "Prophet Without Honor? The Reverend Jesse Jackson and the Palestinian Question," *Journal of Religious Thought* 43, no. 2 (Fall–Winter 1986–87): 51–62, for a similar point of view when considering the controversy over Jackson's position on the Middle East.

2. Barbara A. Reynolds, *Jesse Jackson: The Man, the Movement, the Myth* (Chicago: Nelson-Hall, 1975), 95.

3. Ibid.

4. "Rhodesian Type Arrangement in Chicago," Universal Press Syndicate, January 6, 1980.

5. "Appearance vs. Reality in Higher Education," Universal Press Syndicate, January 13, 1980.

6. "What Was Not Discussed in Iowa," Universal Press Syndicate, January 27, 1980, and "Black Agenda for 1980 Elections," Universal Press Syndicate, February 10, 1980.

7. "Preventing Future Iranian Crises," Universal Press Syndicate, January 20, 1980, and "The Limits of a Military Response," Universal Press Syndicate, February 3, 1980.

8. "Gulf States Support Palestinian Cause," Universal Press Syndicate, February 17, 1980.

9. "Student Power and the Presidency," Universal Press Syndicate, February 24, 1980.

10. This is the principal charge made by Thomas Landess and Richard Quinn in *Jesse Jackson and the Politics of Race* (Ottawa, Ill.; Jameson Books, 1985); see esp. chap. 8, pp. 237–58.

11. See, for example, Media and Presidential Campaigns Issues Forum, University of Missouri–Columbia Journalism School, April 16, 1984.

12. Gunnar Myrdal, *An American Dilemma: The Negro Problem and Modern Democracy*, 2 vols. (New York: Harper & Brothers, 1944), 1:28.

13. See "In Search of a New Focus and a New Vision," 99, and "We Must Act, Not Just React: The Present Challenge of Our Democracy," 39, in *Straight from the Heart*, by Jesse L. Jackson, ed. Roger D. Hatch and Frank E. Watkins (Philadelphia: Fortress Press, 1987).

14. "The Quest for a Just Society and a Peaceful World," Presidential Announcement Speech, Washington, D.C., November 3, 1983.

15. "An Analysis of Our 1980 Political Options and My Conclusions and Endorsement," Operation PUSH Saturday Morning Community Forum, Chicago, September 13, 1980.

16. Martin Luther King, Jr., *Where Do We Go from Here: Chaos or Community?* (New York: Harper & Row, 1967), 4.

17. Ibid., 153.

18. Myrdal, *An American Dilemma,* 1:lxxvii.

19. I have addressed this point at greater length in "Jesse L. Jackson: More Than an Opportunist," *Journal of Religious Thought* 42, no. 2 (Fall–Winter, 1985–86): 73–84.

20. See, for example, "It's Up to You," 205–12, and "Save Our Children: Administrators for Excellence," 194–204, in *Straight from the Heart.*

21. Landess and Quinn make this charge throughout their book, *Jackson and Politics of Race;* see esp. 181–82.

22. "Black Americans Seek Economic Equity and Parity," in *Straight from the Heart,* 281.

23. Robert Kennedy was a strong supporter of Israel, and Sirhan was a displaced Palestinian who opposed Kennedy's views.

24. See "Black Americans Seek Economic Equity and Parity," in *Straight from the Heart,* 280–81.

25. Dennis Farney, "What Makes Jesse Run," *Wall Street Journal,* January 4, 1984.

26. See "The Candidate's Challenge: The Call of Conscience, the Courage of Conviction," in *Straight from the Heart,* 3–18.

27. "The Unfinished Business of the Democratic Convention," Operation PUSH Saturday Morning Community Forum, Chicago, July 28, 1984.

28. Roger Wilkins, "The Natural," *Mother Jones* (August–September 1984): 40.

29. Landess and Quinn, *Jackson and Politics of Race,* 68; see esp. chap. 3, pp. 34–82.

30. See, for example, William Julius Wilson, *The Declining Significance of Race* (Chicago: University of Chicago Press, 1978).

31. Landess and Quinn, *Jackson and Politics of Race,* 257.

32. See, for example, his argument to Charles Murray: "When we saw the devastation in Europe after World War II, we devised the Marshall Plan—a comprehensive, long-term program. Had the Marshall Plan been a five-year investment program—as the War on Poverty essentially was—Europe would have collapsed" ("What Does the Government Owe the Poor?" in *Straight from the Heart,* 262).

33. "It's Up to You," in *Straight from the Heart,* 212.

34. Farney, "What Makes Jesse Run."

35. See, for example, William Safire, "Why Jackson Won't Disavow His Separatist Supporter," *New York Times,* April 10, 1984; Fay S. Joyce,

"Presidential Decision Nears for Jesse Jackson," *New York Times*, September 22, 1983; Julius Lester, "You Can't Go Home Again: Critical Thoughts About Jesse Jackson," *Dissent* (Winter 1985): 21; and Landess and Quinn, *Jackson and Politics of Race*, 192ff.

36. *Time*, April 6, 1970; see esp. pp. 14–23.

37. *Playboy*, November 1969, p. 85.

38. *Ebony*, November 1980, p. 142.

39. See *"Ebony* Interview with the Reverend Jesse L. Jackson," *Ebony*, June 1981, p. 155. The four polls were the Data Black National Opinion Poll and polls of their readers by *Black Enterprise, Ebony*, and *Essence* magazines. Jackson finished second to Young in the *Essence* magazine poll.

40. *"Ebony* Interview with Jackson," 155.

41. King, *Where Do We Go from Here*, 152, 154.

42. Ibid., 157.

43. See "Binding Up the Wounds," in *Straight from the Heart*, 132–36.

44. Press release, June 28, 1984.

45. See "Binding Up the Wounds," in *Straight from the Heart*, 132–36; and ABC-TV's "Nightline," April 27, 1984.

46. Adolph L. Reed, Jr., *The Jesse Jackson Phenomenon: The Crisis of Purpose in Afro-American Politics* (New Haven: Yale University Press, 1986), chap. 7.

47. Ibid., 102.

48. Ibid., 96.

49. Ibid., 98.

50. Ibid., 101.

51. Ibid., 102.

52. For an account of Jackson's position on the Middle East, see chap. 4, pp. 69–70. Note that Jackson calls for *both* Israel and the Palestinians to recognize each other's right to exist in a sovereign and secure homeland.

53. Reed, *Jackson Phenomenon*, 102.

54. See, for example, "The Candidate's Challenge," in *Straight from the Heart*, 4.

55. Preface, in *Straight from the Heart*, ix.

56. See "Binding Up the Wounds," in *Straight from the Heart*, 132–36, for his initial apology. This speech, given at Temple Adath Yeshurun in Manchester, N.H., on February 26, 1984, was devoted exclusively to this issue.

57. Ibid., 135.

58. Coolidge, "Prophet Without Honor."

59. Ibid., 54–55.

60. Ibid., 55. See also Cornel West, "Jesse Jackson's Campaign: Black Politics Will Never Be the Same," *Christianity and Crisis* 13 (August 1984): 303.

61. Coolidge, "Prophet Without Honor," 55.

62. Ibid., 56.

63. Ibid., 56–57.

64. Ibid., 59.

65. Robert Michael Franklin, "Religious Belief and Political Activism in America," *Journal of Religious Thought* 43, no. 2 (Fall–Winter 1986–87): 69, 70.

66. "Meet the Press," NBC-TV, May 24, 1987.

67. Ibid.

68. See "Political Votes, Economic Oats," given January 20, 1978, printed in *Straight from the Heart*, 23–36.

69. See "We Must Act, Not Just React," given June 11, 1978, printed in *Straight from the Heart*, 37–47.

70. See, for example, "Political Votes, Economic Oats," 23, and "We Must Act, Not Just React," 37, in *Straight from the Heart*.

71. "The Candidate's Challenge," in *Straight from the Heart*, 3.

72. "A Call to Action," Operation PUSH Saturday Morning Community Forum, Chicago, June 16, 1979.

73. "From Battleground to Common Ground to Higher Ground," in *Straight from the Heart*, 143.

74. "The Unfinished Business of the Democratic Convention," July 28, 1984.

75. "The Keys to a Democratic Victory in 1984," Thirteenth Annual Convention of Operation PUSH, Chicago, June 7, 1984.

76. "We Must Act, Not Just React," in *Straight from the Heart*, 38.

77. "Political Votes, Economic Oats," in *Straight from the Heart*, 25.

78. "We Must Act, Not Just React," in *Straight from the Heart*, 38.

79. As a prelude to the 1980 primaries, Jackson issued a position paper entitled, "Why We Need a Third Political Force," in which he argued that the existing political options already were too narrow and were threatening to become even more narrow as the country shifted to the right. "A third political force," he concluded, "must emerge around the theme 'Jobs and Justice' that will entice both parties and all political candidates to compete for our agenda and our vote. All politicians will respond to a political constituency. Our challenge is to build and surface such a constituency. . . . Who will constitute this 'third political force'? The black, the Hispanic, the youth, progressive labor, women, environmentalists, the poor, the dispossessed, the oppressed, and all those seeking a more just, humane, and peaceful society and world."

80. "Politics as an Educational Forum," Ford Hall Forum, Boston, March 27, 1983.

81. "Today's Challenge: More Action and a New Direction," Fourteenth Annual Convention of Operation PUSH, Memphis, July 17, 1985.

82. "Forty Years Later—Liberation, But Not Yet Joy," in *Straight from the Heart*, 251–53 passim.

EPILOGUE

1. "From Battleground to Common Ground to Higher Ground," in *Straight from the Heart*, by Jesse L. Jackson, ed. Roger D. Hatch and Frank E. Watkins (Philadelphia: Fortress Press, 1987), 140.

2. Ibid.

3. "Service and a New World Order," in *Straight from the Heart*, 84.

4. Sheila D. Collins, *The Rainbow Challenge: The Jackson Campaign and the Future of U.S. Politics* (New York: Monthly Review Press, 1986), 19.

5. W. E. B. DuBois, *The Souls of Black Folk* (Greenwich, Conn.: Fawcett Books, 1961; originally published in 1903), 22.

Index